W. H. Cologan

The Church of Old England

being a collection of papers bearing on the continuity of the Church in England, and on attempts to justify the Anglican position. Vol. 2

W. H. Cologan

The Church of Old England
being a collection of papers bearing on the continuity of the Church in England, and on attempts to justify the Anglican position. Vol. 2

ISBN/EAN: 9783337264123

Printed in Europe, USA, Canada, Australia, Japan

Cover: Foto ©Lupo / pixelio.de

More available books at **www.hansebooks.com**

The Church of Old England:

A Collection of Papers bearing on the Continuity of the Church in England, and on the attempts to justify the Anglican position.

VOL. II.

LONDON:
CATHOLIC TRUTH SOCIETY,
18 WEST SQUARE, S.E.
DEPÔTS: 21 WESTMINSTER BRIDGE ROAD, S.E.;
245 BROMPTON ROAD, S.W.; 22 PATERNOSTER ROW, E.C.

1895.

CONTENTS.

Henry VIII. and the English Monasteries. By Cardinal Manning.

Papal Supremacy and Infallibility. By the Rev. Sydney F. Smith, S.J.

The Bible and the Reformation. By C. F. B. Allnatt.

Was Barlow a Bishop? By Serjeant Bellasis.

Before and after Gunpowder Plot. By E. Healy Thompson.

189: or, the Church of Old England protests. By the Rev. J. D. Breen, O.S.B.

The Faith of the Ancient English Church concerning the Holy Eucharist. By the Very Rev. Provost Northcote.

King Henry VIII. and the Royal Supremacy.

Popery on every Coin of the Realm.

A Letter to the Working Men of England.

Uniform with the present Volume.
THE CHURCH OF OLD ENGLAND.
VOL. I. *Containing:—*
The Church of Old England. By the Rev. J. D. Breen, O.S.B.
The Continuity of the English Church. By the Very Rev. Canon Croft.
The Popes and the English Church. By Rev. W. Waterworth.
A Voice from the Dead; being a letter to an Anglican Friend, by the Count de Montalembert. [Church in England.
"Church Defence," or Notes on the History of the Catholic
  Plain Truths in answer to Transparent Falsehoods
  Was the British Church Roman Catholic?
  The English Church always Roman Catholic.
  How Henry VIII. robbed England of the Faith.
  Popery in the First Century.
  The Four Doctors.
  The Reformation under Queen Elizabeth.
  Church Endowments—Whose are they?

VOL. III. *Containing:—*
The Conversion of England. By H. E. Cardinal Vaughan.
Rome's Witness against Anglican Orders. By the Rev. Sydney F. Smith, S.J. [Gatty, F.S.A.
The Revival of the Catholic Faith in England. By C. T.
Why I left the Church of England. By James Britten, Hon. Sec. C.T.S.
Before and after the Reformation.
The Foreign and English "Reformation."
Why should we remember the Fifth of November?
The Truth about the Reformation. [Bridgett, C.SS.R.
England's Title: Our Lady's Dowry. By the Rev. T. E.

VOL. IV. *Containing:*
Blessed Peter and the English People. By Cardinal Vaughan.
How "the Church of England washed her Face." By the Rev. Sydney F. Smith, S.J.
The Faith of the Ancient English Church concerning the Blessed Virgin. By the Very Rev. Provost Northcote.
Points on Anglican Controversy:—
  1. "Securus Judicat Orbis Terrarum."
  2. The Reunion of Christendom.
  3. "The Bishop in the Church and the Church in the Bishop."
  4. The Unity of the Church.
The Church of God vindicated by Non-Catholics. 1. Marks of the Church. By H. Morden Bennett, M.A.
How I came Home. By Lady Herbert.
Steps to the Church.
An Appeal to Anglicans.
A House divided against itself. [Church.
"The Church Defence Institution" and the Early English
Archbishop Benson and "The New Italian Mission."
Does an Anglican "forsake the Church of his Baptism" by becoming a Roman Catholic?
Are they Priests?
The Branch Theory.
Twelve Facts proving that the English Church before the Reformation was Roman Catholic.
Continuity Reconsidered. By J. Hobson Matthews.

Henry VIII.
AND
The English Monasteries.*
BY CARDINAL MANNING.

DE MAISTRE said truly that history for three hundred years has been in conspiracy against the Catholic Church. The Protestant historians of Germany, France, England and Scotland, have written a mass of falsified history and falsified biography which reigned supreme and unchallenged until our day. A reaction at last set in. In Germany, Schlegel, Hurter, Ranke, Döllinger, and many more; in France, Montalembert, Ozanam, de Broglie, Rohrbacher, and others; in England, Lingard, Tytler, Hallam, and Friedmann, have broken the spell of historical falsehood. Maitland, in his book on the Dark Ages, was the first to expose the persistent unfaithfulness of anti-Catholic historians, who handed on, with continual embellishment and exaggeration, a multitude of traditional fables. Perhaps no greater example of this immoral practice can be found than in the history of the dissolution of the monasteries in England.

We propose in this paper, following Fr. Gasquet's excellent work on Henry VIII. and the English Monasteries (from which the passages cited in these pages are taken), to give what seems to be a faithful account of the dissolution and of the character of its chief authors,

* Reprinted by permission from the *Dublin Review*, April, 1888.

commencing our task by tracing out the series of events which rendered possible the acts of Henry VIII. First amongst these was the vast change which passed upon the social state of England by the ravages of the Black Death. Though one hundred and fifty years had elapsed before Henry VIII. came to the throne, nevertheless its effects were still perceptible. In the years 1348-9 about one half of the entire population were swept away. In Norwich alone, 57,304 people, besides religious and beggars, and 863 incumbents of livings, were said to have died. Out of 799 priests in the county of Norfolk 527 died of the plague. The bishop obtained from Clement VI. power to dispense with sixty clerks who were then only twenty-one years of age, and allow them to hold livings; a thousand livings had been rendered vacant; two-thirds of the clergy of England had been carried off by the Black Death. The effect of this was to produce a crisis between the labourers and their employers. The permanent retainers of the nobles and the monasteries had disappeared, and the modern system of letting had been introduced. Peasant proprietors were greatly reduced in number, and the people were no longer bound to the lords of the land by the old ties. This destroyed the power of the nobles and exalted that of the king. The poverty and distress following upon the diminution of labour and of agriculture, and the suspension of religious care and teaching caused by the sudden removal of a great multitude of the clergy, had disastrous effects. Upon this followed all the evils of thirty-five years of warfare between the Houses of York and Lancaster. The power of the nobles was finally broken, and the power of the king became sole and supreme. Two evils followed upon this. First, the creation of new peers in the fifteenth and sixteenth centuries, who had no sympathy, by birth or training, with the traditions of the past; and secondly, the rise of a new race of men—namely, the "Officials," adventurers, ill-paid, restless, discontented and grasping. Their whole hope and dependence was in the king, and they became ready tools of his despotic will.

All these preludes made possible such a career as that

of Thomas Wolsey. As the favourite of the king, and Lord High Chancellor of England, he gradually clothed himself with all the powers of the State, and by the favour of the king he obtained all the highest powers of the Church, one only excepted. He was Archbishop of York, and held Winchester and other bishoprics *in commendam*, together with the Abbey of St. Albans. He was Cardinal and Legate, and, during the imprisonment of Clement VIII., he obtained faculties for himself and for the King of France to confirm all kinds of ecclesiastical matters with a *quasi* papal authority. For the first time in the history of England such civil and ecclesiastical powers were united in one person. The transfer of the same as a whole afterwards to Henry VIII., followed almost as a matter of course by the Statute of 1534.

It must not be forgotten that at this time the minds of men had been distracted by the great Western Schism, by the frequent subtraction of obedience, by the doubtful election of Popes, and the simultaneous existence of two or even three claimants to the Holy See, that the supreme Pontifical authority had become in many places a matter of academical discussion. Nothing but such preludes could have instigated even Gerson to write on thesis *de Auferibilitate Papæ*. This throws much light upon the singular fact attested by Sir Thomas More, in speaking to the jury and the judge by whom he was condemned, when the verdict of death was brought in against him:—"I have, by the grace of God, been always a Catholic, never out of communion with the Roman Pontiff; but I have heard it said at times that the authority of the Roman Pontiff was certainly lawful and to be respected, but still an authority derived from human law and not standing upon a divine prescription. Then, when I observed that public affairs were so ordered that the sources of the power of the Roman Pontiff would necessarily be examined, I gave myself up to a most diligent examination of that question for the space of seven years, and found that the authority of the Roman Pontiff, which you rashly—I will not use stronger language—have set aside, is not only lawful, to be respected and necessary, but also grounded on the divine law and prescription. That is my opinion; that is the belief in which by the grace of God I shall die." Already in those days the name Papist was used as a reproach.

Wolsey was the first at that time to set example of suppressing monasteries, for the purpose of founding a college at Oxford. The king followed his example, in asking to suppress monasteries for the foundation of new cathedrals. Men were, therefore, prepared for such a policy.

Whatever faults may be charged against the career of Wolsey, there is a grandeur about it, both in his prosperity and in his fall. Few things in our history are more pathetic than the suddenness with which he fell. The tyranny of Henry VIII. was oriental. His favour was life, his displeasure death. Surrounded by enemies, watched day and night by spies, betrayed by those he trusted most, the great Cardinal and Chancellor found himself in a day stripped of all power, banished from court, and a prisoner in his own house. Mr. Brewer has written this history with a worthy compassion. The few months of Wolsey in the Archbishopric of York, visiting his churches, confirming children, and living among the poor, were a beautiful picture of Christian humility, and the best preparation for the end that awaited him at Leicester on the way to the Tower. The fall of Wolsey was the fall of an ecclesiastical period. The next Lord High Chancellor of England was Thomas More, and with him came in the lay world, which has reigned more and more until this day. It is strange that the first layman that kept the king's conscience should have died a martyr for resisting the royal lusts.

The martyrdom of Blessed Thomas More made way for a man as bad and as base as the king and the times demanded.

Thomas Crumwell is said to have been the son of a blacksmith at Putney. He was, it seems, for some offence, thrown into prison, and obliged to leave the country. Then he was a common soldier in Italy. He was, as it was believed, in the army of the Duke of Bourbon, which in 1527 sacked Rome and imprisoned Clement VII. It

the English Monasteries. 5

is said that among those who outraged Rome was "an Englishman of low, vicious habits and infidel principles, who afterwards became of terrific importance in the Church of England." Crumwell told Cranmer "that he had been at one time a ruffian." Then he became a merchant, a scrivener, a money-lender, a lawyer, a member of Parliament, a courtier and dependent of Wolsey, a dealer in "Boston pardons," and a disciple of Machiavelli, whose works he studied while he was in Italy, The history of his rise and iniquities verifies the Italian proverb—

Inglese Italianato
E Diavolo Incarnato.

Henry VIII., when at cards, if a knave was dealt to him, used to say, "I have Crumwell."

When Wolsey fell, Crumwell had to take care of himself, for the people had already consigned him to the gallows. It was believed that he saved himself by destroying his master—that is, by stealing and delivering to the king the royal permisson, under the great seal, whereby Wolsey had exercised his legatine powers. Certain it is that Wolsey, not being able to produce this document, was in *præmunire*, and compelled to throw himself on the king's mercy. This was final and fatal. All the Cardinal's possessions were forfeited, but Crumwell retained, by royal leave, the administration of them. In this office he made himself profitable to certain nobles; and from that time his rise was rapid. He became Master of the Jewels, Chancellor of the Exchequer, Master of the Rolls, Secretary of State, Vicar-General of the king in ecclesiastical matters, Lord Privy Seal, Dean of Wells, High Chamberlain. In 1533 he was knighted, then made Earl of Essex. In 1534 the king had made himself, by Act of Parliament, Head of the Church in all matters spiritual and temporal. In all this usurped power Thomas Crumwell was Vicar-General, and, in fact, the sole executive of this twofold supremacy, ecclesiastical and civil.

The suppression of monasteries was, as we know, no new thing in England. Edward I. and Edward II. seized the alien priories; Edward III. re-established them, but took

them into his own hand: Henry V. finally suppressed
them all. William of Wykham founded New College with
ecclesiastical property. Winchester, Eton, and King's
College, Cambridge, were likewise endowed by suppressed
religious houses. Out of suppressed houses Chicheley
endowed All Souls in Oxford; Waynfleet founded Magdalen College; Bishop Alcock founded Jesus College,
in Cambridge. Bishop Fisher advised the dissolution of
Brome Hall, in the diocese of Salisbury, and Lillechurch,
in his own diocese of Rochester; but all these suppressions were made with the sanction of the Holy See. In
like manner afterwards, Wolsey suppressed many monasteries for the purpose of founding Christ Church in Oxford
and a College in Ipswich. Henry VIII. at first opposed
Wolsey's suppressions, but afterwards, to supply his own
needs, followed his example; and this he carried out by
the instrumentality of Thomas Crumwell. Wolsey had
before employed Thomas Crumwell with Dr. Allen for
the same purpose, so that the work was not new to him.
But he added to it all the aggravations of corruption,
cruelty, and hypocrisy. The royal treasury was empty,
and no readier source for its replenishment than the robbery of the monasteries was at hand. The Vicar-General,
therefore, in the year 1535, began by issuing injunctions,
which it was impossible for the monasteries to accept, for
the purpose of driving them either to rebellion or to surrender. The first article of these injunctions was the
acknowledgment of the king's headship over the Church.
Finding the Carthusians and the Franciscans firm in refusing this act of apostacy, every form of persecution,
from the intrusion of strangers into their community, the
violation of rule, the sowing of dissension between subjects and superiors, and finally imprisonment with torture,
the rack, and the axe, were inflicted on them.

Then for the visitation of monasteries throughout England four memorable persons were appointed by Crumwell
as his agents—viz., Layton, Legh, Ap Rice, and London.
The insolence, avarice, and servility of these men are
proved by their own letters to Crumwell, of which sufficient proofs will be given hereafter.

When this iniquitous mockery of a visitation was drawing to a close, the Parliament was assembled to carry the Act of Suppression. The writs for the election of members were sent out with the name of the persons to be elected. In the election at Canterbury two burgesses were returned contrary to the pleasure of the king, and the mayor was compelled to cancel the election, and to send the two royal nominees. In like manner, in summoning the House of Lords, peers that were not of the king's mind were passed over. Tunstall, Bishop of Durham, was advised, on account of his age and infirmities, not to expose himself to the long journey from Durham. Nevertheless, he set out, but on his way was met by a royal letter that sent him home again. But even this packed Parliament would not do the king's pleasure :—

On Saturday in Ember week the King's Grace came in among the Burgesses of the Parliament, and delivered them a Bill, and bade them look upon it, and weigh it in conscience. He would not, he said, have them pass it nor any other thing, because his Grace giveth them the Bill, but they to see to it if it be for the common weal to his subjects, and have an eye thitherward, and on Wednesday next he will be there again to hear their minds.

The preamble of the Bill asserts that, in consideration of the evil lives of those in the smaller monasteries, " the King's Most Royal Majesty . . . . . having knowledge that the premises be true, as well as by the *compertes* of his late Visitation, as by sundry credible informations; considering also that divers and great solemn monasteries of this realm, wherein, thanks be to God, religion is right well kept and observed, &c. . . . . Whereupon the said Lords and Commons, by a great deliberation finally be resolved that it is, shall be much more to the pleasure of Almighty God that the property of those Religious should be converted to better use, and the unthrifty persons so spending the same should be compelled to reform their lives;" therefore they pray the King to take all the property of monasteries having an income of under £200 a year. And even this limited submission was not obtained without threats which destroyed all liberty of action. Sir Henry Spelman tells us as follows :—

> It is true the Parliament gave them (*i.e.*, the monasteries) to him, but so unwillingly, as I have heard, that when the Bill had stuck long in the Lower House, and could get no passage, he commanded the Commons to attend him in the forenoon in his gallery, where he let them wait till late in the afternoon ; and then coming out of his chamber, walking a turn or two among them, and looking angrily upon them, first on the one side and then on the other. "At last I hear," sayth he, "that my Bill will not pass, or I will have some of your heads."

And here we have an example of a tradition which has been handed on without hesitation and with much embellishment by anti-Catholic writers, for which no foundation in history can be found. It has been said by all writers, from Burnett to Dean Stanley, that the "Black Book," detailing the crimes of the monasteries, was laid before the Parliament in the Chapter House of Westminster. Dean Stanley tells us "that on the table of the Chapter House was placed the famous 'Black Book, which sealed the fate of all the monasteries of England, and sent a thrill of horror through the House of Commons when they heard it." Now, no such book has ever been found, and there is not a shred of contemporary evidence to prove that such a "Black Book" ever existed. The preamble of the Act of Suppression cites the "knowledge of the king, the *compertes* of the Visitation, and credible informations." The following is the summary of the evidence against the monasteries :—

> In the *comperta* and letters which report as to the monasteries of a considerable portion of England, scarcely 250 monks and nuns are named as guilty of incontinence. In the same districts the religious must have numbered many thousands. Of these 250, more than a third part can be identified as having subsequently received pensions upon the dissolution of their houses, a fact which even Burnett would consider as disproving the charge in their regard. Of the entire number of convents of women visited and reported upon by Layton and Legh in the North, they are able to relate very little amiss. Only some twenty-seven nuns in all are charged with vice, and of these, seventeen are known to have been afterwards pensioned. Further, in their whole visitation, extending over thirteen counties, they only report

that some fifty men and two women were anxious to abandon the religious life, even under the restrictions imposed by Crumwell's injunctions.

This summary accumulates the worst that can be found in the Reports of the Visitors. All those, who have had experience of what popular allegations are worth, will know how to estimate the figures and the charges above given. But where in all this is the "Black Book?"

The wealth of the English monasteries was undoubtedly great. It had accumulated for centuries by the gifts of the devout as their free-will offerings, and of the penitent in reparation for their sins, and for the relief of the poor. The monasteries were a thousand in number, and they possessed a third of the land in England. In the reign of Edward I. the soil of England consisted of 67,000 knights' fees, of which ecclesiastics held about 28,000. They were as a rule good and kind landlords. It was a proverb that "it was better to be under the crosier than under the lance." The tenants of the abbeys and priories were a contented race; and the abbey gate was ever open to the needs and the sufferings of the poor. It is a mistake to say that the poor were provided for by the doles of the monasteries, for they were to be found only in a third of the land of England. But they were a thousand centres of constant beneficence; and in the other two-thirds of the land, the palaces of the bishops, the homes of the clergy, the castles of the nobles, and the houses of the faithful, maintained all the year round the Christian law of almsgiving. There was poverty in England, because there were old age and sickness, and the vicissitudes of life and fortune. But there was everywhere the faith which honoured the poor as the brethren of Christ, and the charity which spontaneously ministered to Him in them. Then came the robbery of God and His poor. By the Act of Suppression:—

The monasteries were given to the King and his heirs only "in as ample a manner" as they were possessed by the religious superiors. These were trustees for common purposes and never regarded their property in any other light than as held for the support of religion and the poor. Further, the purpose for which the monastic property was diverted by this Act from its possessors and given to the King is stated to be "that his Highness may lawfully give, grant, and dispense them or any of them at his will or pleasure to the honour of God and the wealth of this realm." .... It was further enacted that on the site of every dissolved religious house the new possessor should be bound, under heavy penalties, to provide hospitality and service of the poor, such as had been given them previously by the religious foundations. .... The repudiation of these rights of the needy by those who became possessed of the confiscated property is one of the greatest blots on our national history. It has caused the spoliation of monastery and convent to be regarded as the rising of the rich against the poor.*

It has been the fashion of political economists to describe the demoralization of the poor by the alms of the monasteries, and to cite in proof the statutes against "sturdy beggars" and the like; but we have it upon a high economical authority "that the fifteenth century and the first quarter of the sixteenth were the golden age of the English labourer, if we are to interpret the wages which he earned by the cost of the necessaries of life." When the greater monasteries had been plundered and wrecked, and the Church had been robbed, the poverty of England began. The faith and charity, that is the Christianity, of the people had so rapidly declined as to need the intervention of public law. The bishops and clergy were commanded to stir up the charity of the rich to help the poor; but with so little result that an Act of Parliament, 5 Eliz. c. 3, made the relief of the poor compulsory, and England for the first time had a Poor Law. For two centuries this law was administered with a recognition of its natural justice, but for the last fifty years it has been the butt of all kind of denouncement. Nevertheless it has saved the land laws of England until now, and perhaps few are conscious how powerfully but surely it has guarded our social peace. The foresight of St. Thomas of Canterbury made him defend the goods of the Church as the patrimony of the poor. We see at this day the twofold poverty, temporal and spiritual, which the Tudors

* "Six Centuries of Work and Wages" (p. 326), by James Thorold Rogers.

the English Monasteries. 11

inflicted upon the people of England. It was not so much the Church as the poor whom they robbed of their inheritance.

Crumwell's tyranny lasted eight years. His account book shows the immense wealth accumulated by private and public extortion. "Archbishops, bishops, abbots, priors, nobles, commoners, officials, unknown laymen, towns, colleges, cathedral chapters, all sent fees and new year's donations to propitiate the favour of the great man." For instance, in January, 1539, £9,000—gifts of £10, £50, and £300, £100, and £266, came from all over the country; for the elections at Fountains, Gisboro, Whitby, and many other places, large bribes are offered for nominations. If he will make a certain monk Abbot of Vale Royal, "he will be contented," writes Sir Piers Dutton, "to give you £100 in hand, and further to do you as much pleasure as any man shall." William Penison wishes to be Receiver at the dissolution of Reading Abbey, and presents a diamond, "set in a gold ring, meet to be set in the breast of a George." The Abbot of Miravale writes that he learns from Dr. Legh that "Crumwell is looking for the £40 promised to you, for his trouble in my regard. I have already paid £100." The Abbot of Pipwell "will do all that a poor man can to gratify your lordship with £200." To avert the dissolution of Colchester he was offered £24,000. The Abbot of Leicester sends £40. His successor had to pay a yearly tax of £240—and so on for pages. As for presents : of a brace of fat oxen, and a score of fat wethers; fish from Croyland; apples from King's Langley; partridges and pheasants from Harrow; Irish hawks from Bath; and £40 from one John Hunter "towards furnishing your cellar with wine" in recompense for Crumwell's part in a law case relating to the property of John Hunter's wife. Then again "money in a purse," "in a white leather purse," "in a crimson sateen purse," "in a handkerchief," "in a glove," "at Arundel in a glove," "in a pair of gloves under a cushion in the middle window of the gallery." "A chain melted for my lord worth more than £5,000." His note-book shows as follows : " Item, to remember

Warren for one monastery. Mr. Gostwyke for a monastery. John Freeman for Spalding. Mr. Kingsmill for Wherwell. *Myself* for Lunde. Item, to remember John Godsall for something for he hath need; and Item, to remember to know the true value of the goods at Castle Acre *for my part thereof*."

Then follow cups and ewers and trenchers of gold, platters and dishes and salters of silver by the dozen, and the gold cross of St. Albans, worth £106. But this is endless. Maitland writes that he was "the great patron of ribaldry, and the protector of the ribald, of the low jester, of the filthy ballad-monger, of the ale-house singers and hypocritical mockers at feasts—in short, of all the blasphemous mocking and scoffing which disgraced the Protestant party at the time of the Reformation."

The fall of Wolsey was full of dignity, and moved men to compassion. The fall of Crumwell had no sign of dignity, and no man wept for him. We have it in all its details. "By a Nemesis of fate he passed to the scaffold suddenly and almost untried, and certainly unheard in his own defence." This was probably by an Act devised or obtained by himself.

On June 11, 1540, the French Ambassador wrote that he had heard, an hour before sending his despach, that Crumwell had been sent to the Tower. On June 23 he gave full information. He says that Crumwell was altogether unprepared for his downfall. When the Lieutenant of the Tower entered the Council Chamber at Westminster, and informed him that he was ordered to take him prisoner, Crumwell, moved with indignation, threw his hat on the floor. Some one of the Council called out that he was a traitor, and must be judged by the laws he had himself made. The Duke of Norfolk tore the Order of St. George from his neck, and the Garter was also taken from him. Before the news spread he was already in the Tower, and the people knew of his arrest by seeing the king's officers enter to search his house. By the next day the king had already begun to distribute his fallen favourite's offices, and sent an officer through the streets of London, publicly forbidding any man to call him Lord Privy Seal, or by any other title or dignity, but simply Thomas Crumwell, cloth carder; saying that the king had taken from him every privilege and title of nobility which he had ever granted him. His attainder declares him to be a false and corrupt traitor, selling for manifold sums of money various grants, even to foreigners and aliens. And further, that as Vicegerent under the Great Seal, he licensed divers persons, detected and suspected of heresy, openly to preach and teach, saying that he would fight even against the king to maintain these heresies. His arrest was so sudden that he could destroy no papers. On the morning of June 10, 1540, he was supreme in England; in the evening he was in the Tower. On June 28 he was brought to the scaffold on Tower Hill.

Such was the end of the master; it only remains to give the end of the minions. They had not even the dignity of the axe. These were Dr. Richard Layton, Thomas Legh, John Ap Rice, and Dr. John London. "It is not impossible," says Mr. Blunt, a Protestant, in his 'History of the Reformation,' "that even such bad men may have told the truth in this matter. But the character of witnesses must always form an important element in estimating the value of their testimony, and the character of such obscene, profligate, and perjured witnesses as Layton and London, could not well be worse. These men were not just Lots, vexed with the filthy conversation of the wicked, but filthy dreamers, who defiled the flesh, despised ecclesiastical dominion, and spake evil of dignitaries in the very spirit of the Evil One."

Dr. Layton was a pluralist by the favour of Crumwell. Crumwell was invited by him to his rectory at Harrow in these words: "Surely, Simeon was never so glad to see Christ, his Master, as I shall be to see your lordship." He offered Crumwell £100 to make him Chancellor of the Diocese of Salisbury; and when made Dean of York, he pawned the plate belonging to the Minster.

It is evident from Layton's letters to Crumwell that he had made up his mind beforehand what he intended to find in the monasteries that he visited. Moreover, it was absolutely impossible, in the time given by the visitors, to hold any inquiry, worthy of the name, in the numberless monasteries, especially in the North, which were visited in the most hurried way. The insolence, violence, and falsehood of Layton and Legh made the Pilgrims of Grace demand their instant and condign punishment.

Next we find Dr. Layton scampering over Sussex, and writing to Crumwell as follows: "On Friday night I came into Sussex to an abbey called Durtford, it might better be called Dirtyford. Then to an abbey .... towards Chichester, because of their poverty not able to lodge. These two poor priories we will dispatch on Monday by the way. And so on Monday at night we shall be at Chichester." He then describes his treatment of the Abbot of Waverley. He took away the keys of office from all the monks, and made new officers, "perchance as stark knaves as the others. It shall be expedient for you to give the Abbot a lesson, and tell the poor fool what he should do amongst the monks."

Of the monastery of Lewes, Layton reports: "At Lewes I found the monks morally bad and traitors, and having intimidated the Prior on his knees with the worst words I could devise, I ordered him to appear before you, and you will be able to do what you like with him."

From Lewes he went to Battle. He writes as follows: "The Abbot of Battle is the varast hayne bette, and buserde and the arants chorle that ever I see. In all other places whereat I come, especially the black sort of devilish monks, I am sorry to know as I do. Surely, I thynk they be past amendment, and that God hath utterly withdrawn his grace from them."

Dr. Layton sums up his own worth: "Praying God that rather I may be buried quick than to be the occasion why the King's Highness should diminish any part of the affiance of your proved mind towards His Grace."

So much for Dr Layton—by his own showing, a bad, insolent, and unjust man.

We come next to Dr. Legh.

Ap Rice will save us trouble. He wrote to Crumwell a full indictment against his fellow commissioner. "First

in his going he is too insolent and pompatique . . . .
Then he handleth the Fathers when he cometh very roughly
. . . . The man is young and of an intolerable elation
of mind. . . . . For the election of the Prior of Coventry
he took £15—at Revel £20, besides his costs, which is,
in my opinion, too much. . . . . He maketh them to send
after him such rewards as may please him." He went
about with twelve men in livery besides his brother. After
sending this letter, Ap Rice was frightened, and wrote next
day to Crumwell, begging him not to tell Dr. Legh.
" Forasmuch as the said Mr. Doctor is of such acquain-
tance and familiarity with many rufflers and serving men
. . . . and I have commonly no great assistance with me
when I go abroad, might take perchance irrecoverable
harm of him or of his ere I were aware. Please keep secret
what I have said."

Sanders, writing almost at that time, says: " Lee (Legh),
indeed, in order to discharge correctly the duties laid upon
him, tempted the religious to sin, and he was more ready
to inquire into, and to speak about, uncleanness of living
than anything else."

No wonder the nuns were terrified at " Mr. Doctor Legh,"
the familiar of rufflers, a prurient talker, an accuser, if not
also a tempter, of the innocent.

As to Ap Rice, little need be said. He had the reputation of an unfrocked priest. Legh accused him of some
discreditable acts, and it appears that he never received any
spiritual promotion for his services.

Dr. John London's case may be speedily summed up.
Even Cranmer called him "the stout and filthy preben-
dary of Windsor." He and one Simons, a lawyer, "that
set traps for others, were catched at length themselves."
They were condemned to ride through Windsor, Reading,
and Newbury, their faces to the tails of their horses, and
to stand in the pillory on a market-day with a paper on their
heads proclaiming their offence.

Once more Mr. Blunt, with his usual justice, says: "A
dean, twice detected in immorality and put to open penance
for it, and afterwards convicted of perjury, is not the
stuff of which credible witnesses are made."

We have learned the worth of this precious quaternion from two safe sources—first, from their own words; and next, from what they said of each other.

Fuller says that the Catholics accused the visitors of employing profligate young men to tempt the nuns to sin, and tells a story of two young men going to a convent near Cambridge, but without success.

Mr. Blunt says again ('Reformation,' i. 316):

"The story has too much *vraisemblance* to be set aside. And in addition to this, the tone of Layton's letters to Crumwell are of such a kind, as to make one fear that some nuns were, indeed, wickedly seduced, and others not less wickedly accused falsely. Those, however, who duly appreciate the character of their country-women, will believe that among these evil-entreated innocents there were not a few who passed through the scorching fire of temptation scathless, under the protection of their heavenly bridegroom. For the English daughters of the nineteenth century, whom we see around us, are sisters to the English nuns of the sixteenth, of whom we know only by vague tradition."

Such then is the impeachment of Thomas Crumwell and his associates. If ever men were self-condemned, they are. Yet it was upon the evidence of such wretches that the highest sanctity and the noblest intellects of England were blackened and martyred. But upon the oaths of such men no just man would take even the life of a dog.

Papal Supremacy and Infallibility.

BY THE
REV. SYDNEY F. SMITH, S.J.

I. Papal Supremacy—Can you have Unity without it?

THE Church is by divine appointment a visible society with an external organization binding its members together and placing them under the spiritual government of bishops and clergy.

This much is not only clear beyond a doubt from the Holy Scriptures and the history of the primitive Church, but it is also common ground between Catholics and the High Church section of Anglicans. Anglicans likewise admit that as there is one Baptism, so it is desirable there should be one Faith everywhere professed, and perfect sacramental intercommunion prevailing between the various portions of the world-wide society. Catholics go further, and believe unity of faith and communion to be not only desirable but essential. However in the present papers we must commence from common ground, and therefore I only postulate as a starting point the desirability of these two attributes. Since they are desirable, it may be assumed that God has made provision to secure their maintenance; also we may be sure that such provision will take into account the characteristics of human nature and will be so ordered as to work in harmony with them. The arrangements of God are never violent. Let us then examine the Anglican and the Catholic theories concerning the institution of the Church, with a view to discover whether either of them, and if either, which of them, involves a provision answering to this criterion of divine origin.

According to Anglicans each local Church enjoys independence. It is not quite clear whether they attribute the independence to each diocese or province, or only to each national Church. But that is a question of detail which need not detain us. Although the local churches are separately independent, each owes submission to the Church Universal, and therefore to a General Council, which is the Church Universal assembled in the person of representatives from its constituent dioceses. Hence if a General Council is sitting, it has supreme power to enquire into and settle with authority controversies concerning faith. To its definitions which are infallible the local churches are then bound to render assent, under penalty of separation from the communion of the faithful, and forfeiture of character as duly constituted portions of the Church Universal. General Councils however are not always possible. The earliest was not held till two centuries later than the death of the latest apostle, and the last which any Anglicans acknowledge took place in the ninth century. During the prolonged intervals between successive Councils, the office of determining disputed questions of faith, in default of any common authority, falls to each separate Church. This duty carries with it the further responsibility of deciding whether other local churches have so far corrupted the faith that communion with them can no longer be maintained without sacrifice of the allegiance due to truth: from which it results that if two or more portions of the Church are at variance among themselves as to what is corruption and what is purity of faith, they must interrupt communion until either one party has changed its mind or a General Council has supervened and decided.

Here is the Anglican system. Will it work? Is it calculated to maintain unity? Obviously not, without continual recourse to miracle. The active workings of the human mind are ever raising difficulties against received beliefs, and the history of the Church attests to a continual succession of disputes concerning the nature of God, of the Incarnation, Predestination, Grace, the Sacraments,—in short, concerning the entire range of Christian dogmas. Each age has had its own controversies. Thus the question of intercommunion must inevitably be soon forced to the front. Let us study the matter in the concrete, and for the purpose make the inconceivable supposition that the Churches which own the Pope's supremacy are prepared so far to surrender to Anglican arguments as to disavow it, retaining at the same time their present belief on all other dogmas. The "branches" desire to restore intercommunion, but agreement must first be obtained, and what likelihood is there of this? Anglicans express great confidence in their arguments, and are sure that if once Catholics gave up the Papacy and disengaged themselves from the bias its acknowledgment involves, it would not be long before they abandoned their other errors as well. We Catholics on the other hand are not so impressed by Anglican arguments. We think our own infinitely superior, and theirs in fact to be, with scanty exceptions, no arguments at all, but rather flippant evasions. This same difference would in all probability continue to exist even after the postulated disavowal of Papal authority, and would last till a General Council could be convoked. How soon would this be? The Anglicans and the Greeks have not yet succeeded in assembling a Council among themselves, although there is no Pope to stand between them. Would it be easier for three "branches" to assemble a Council than it is for two? Governments would be likely to intervene, fearful lest the result should brand beliefs rooted in the hearts of their people and should disturb the tranquillity of their realms. There would be quarrels as to the share of the representation to which the Churches were respectively entitled. Should the inferior clergy be represented? should unattached bishops? should one "branch" be allowed to swamp the rest by undue multiplication of its own episcopate? Here surely are hard facts which would delay the meeting for years and perhaps centuries, the undesirable state of interrupted intercommunion being meanwhile forced to endure.

But let us suppose the difficulties at last overcome by

some *Deus ex machinâ* and the Council assembled. Let us even pass over any embarrassments that might arise as to the choice of a president. Provided it were arranged that the president should be a mere chairman, with no voting preponderance over his fellows, it is quite possible this preliminary might be arranged without serious dispute. But now we have the parties face to face, each bringing with it a deep-rooted attachment to its own beliefs and a conscientious conviction that its opponents were in the wrong. There would be plenty of hot blood. When the Pan-Anglican Conference met, although its members were divided among themselves by enormous doctrinal differences, the proceedings nevertheless were consistently decorous and resulted in resolutions. This however was due to the studious care taken not to touch the raw. Propositions were drawn up, either of a colourless character or else conceived like the Thirty-Nine Articles in ambiguous language, and there was much euphemistic talk about large-minded comprehensiveness. But in a General Council the encounter would be real. Comprehensiveness would be at a discount. Ambiguity would have to give place to the nicest accuracy of expression. And then what chance of an agreement? Imagine a Cardinal Manning being won over by the debates to the language of the Thirty-Nine Articles on Justification by Faith and Works of Supererogation; or a Dr. Ryle of Liverpool to the Tridentine doctrine on Indulgences! Out of the impossibility of reaching general agreement through discussion would grow the further dispute whether conciliar authority attached to the voice of the majority or only to that of unanimity. The minority would of course be biassed strongly in favour of the latter alternative. Each side could offer forcible reasons for its own contention. The one side would trace the authority of Councils to the witness they are able to render to the universal prevalence of the dogmas decreed. Such witness, they could urge, involves general, if not absolute unanimity among the assembled Fathers. The others would point to the impossibility of securing unanimity in the very cases which most require authoritative settlement, and would contend that either conciliar authority attaches to the voice of the majority or else that General Councils become a farce. One can see no other outlet from the deadlock than the breaking up of the assembly and the return of its members to their dioceses, more full of excitement and recriminations and more confirmed in their previous opinions than ever. So for instance it was at Ephesus. Anglicans may agree with Catholics in thinking that on that occasion the Nestorians were ejected from the Church and the legitimate voice of the Council expressed by the adherents of St. Cyril. But this was not the Nestorian view; and if we estimate the proceedings by the Anglican theory, one does not see why the Nestorian view was untenable.

Let us now suppose in the teeth of all likelihood that our future Council has terminated in complete agreement and the restoration of communion. How long will it last? Is it not morally certain that before long disputes would arise about the interpretation of the Conciliar Decrees and there would be a recrudescence of the old evil? The causes which produced former differences continuing to exist and to work, would be ever widening the doctrinal chasm till conscience seemed to compel another breach of communion. In short the Anglican system reveals itself as incapable of maintaining Unity. Its inevitable outcome must be at best a perpetual oscillation between the condition of intercommunion and that of schism, or rather interruption of chronic schism by short intervals of intercommunion. According to this system the state of union is for the Church of God the state of *unstable equilibrium.*

Now take the Catholic system. This holds that the Bishop of one particular See—that of Rome—is by Divine appointment the Centre of Unity for the entire Church. All are bound to be in communion with him: any church excommunicated by him ceases *ipso facto* to be a duly constituted member of the whole: it becomes a branch cut off. In pursuance of this radical idea, the Bishop of the Central See has received supreme authority over the whole body, and is further endowed through the special providence of God with the gift of Infallibility, so that the allegiance due to his authority may never be incompatible with the allegiance due to truth. Here is the complete system. Could anything be simpler or more calculated to work with ease? When controversies spring up it lies ultimately with the Supreme Pontiff to decide. The guidance of the Holy Spirit, which secures his decrees from error, is given, not by way of inspiration, but by way of special providence overruling the deliberations which his natural prudence dictates. He is therefore bound to examine and to ponder, to call in the aid of wise counsellors, and, when the crisis demands and the opportunities permit, to convoke a General Council of the Church to sit with him in judgment. But there is no longer any difficulty in securing the proper working of such an assembly. Its members, being bred to unity of faith, are not likely to differ so widely that even unanimity is never an improbable issue of their deliberations: but should this fail, there is no uncertainty as to the side from which the authoritative view comes. It comes from that which can reckon to itself the confirming voice of the Pontiff. So also during the interval between the holding of Councils, there is never any fear or possibility of the Church's Unity being broken. There may indeed be schisms in the sense of portions breaking off from the main body to their own cost. But the Church ever One will always be distinguished from the schismatics, the trunk from the cut-off branch, because the trunk, the Church, is essentially united with its Supreme Pastor. We have compared the condition of Unity amidst the oscillations essential to the Anglican theory to the condition of unstable equilibrium. To compare this same condition of Unity under the Catholic system to that even of stable equilibrium would be to understate. Unity is not so much a condition to which the oscillating body tends to revert, but rather one from which it is impossible for it to depart.

The comparison we have been considering establishes a presumption in favour of the Catholic doctrine of Papal Supremacy and Infallibility. This by itself is important. It renders the existence of solid arguments in proof of the fact highly probable. It ought also, when biblical or patristic passages by reason of any ambiguity are susceptible of a twofold interpretation, one supporting, the other opposed to the dogma, to turn the scale in its favour. Still presumption is not proof: and it therefore still remains to supply proof.

II. St. Peter's Supremacy—Can it be proved from the Bible?

There are three texts in the Bible which Anglicans dislike, viz., St. Matt. xvi. 13-20, St. Luke xxii. 31, 32, St. John xxi. 15-17. Anglican preachers give them a wide berth unless compelled by a challenge from adversaries to discuss them, and then the discussion is of the most summary kind. It partakes more of the character of explaining away than explaining. It is felt to be a case of handling hot coals. Let us hear what the first and the chief of these texts (St. Matt. xvi. 13-20) has to say about the Primacy of St. Peter. The time of our Lord's public ministry was drawing to a close, and it was becoming more and more manifest from the persistent rejection of His authority by the leaders of the Jewish people, that He could not hope to engraft the organization of the Church upon that of the Synagogue. The Church must be established on independent lines. He then began to conclude His Galilean preaching, and withdrawing with his disciples to a secluded region far to the north, He gathered His disciples around Him and by an enquiry concerning the nature of the doctrine which lay at the root of the Gospel dispensation, drew from St. Peter a splendid profession of faith in the Divinity of the Messiah. Our Lord pronounced this apostle blessed, and proceeded to reward his faith by a promise of certain privileges to be conferred upon him. The promise is threefold. He shall be the Rock on which the Church is built, a prerogative already foreshadowed in the change of name given on an earlier occasion (St. John i. 42), for the name Peter means Rock: he shall bear the keys of the kingdom of heaven: he shall receive unlimited power to bind and loose.

These expressions are figurative, and we must ascertain the force of the figure as received among the Jews, before we can reach the ulterior meaning. The office of a rock in regard to the superimposed building is to sustain it; to impart stability to its structure and preserve it from tottering and tumbling before the blast of the tempest or the inrush of the undermining waters. This is clear from the parable concerning the houses built on the sand and the rock respectively (St. Luke vi. 48, 49). Keys are the symbol of rule; or, which comes to much the same, of the power to allow or deny entrance into the city. Compare Apoc. iii. 7, where it is said of our Lord Himself, "Thus saith the Holy and the True One; Who hath the key of David; Who openeth and no man shutteth; Who shutteth and no man openeth" (see also Isaiah xxii. 22). To *bind* and to *loose* signifies to *remit* and *retain* sins, or else to *forbid* and *allow*, that is to *legislate*. The former is the interpretation usual with the Fathers. The latter is considered by some modern scholars more in accordance with the usage of the Jews. We need not concern ourselves with this difficulty; either sense will do. Peter then received from our Lord (for of course the promise was fulfilled to the letter) the office of imparting to the Church a stability which should hold its structure firmly together; the power to admit into it and exclude from it; and lastly a most ample legislative right over its members. It is difficult to see how a plain unprejudiced mind can fail to gather from such language the appointment of St. Peter to the office of Supreme Ruler over the Church. A ruler's office is well described as that of holding together the social organization. Remove him and the parts disintegrate into fragments. To a ruler again belongs the power to admit into and to banish from his kingdom, as also that of making laws for those who are admitted. This interpretation is confirmed by St. John xxi. 15–17 where St. Peter is singled out in the same manner from the rest and told to *feed the sheep*. "To feed his sheep," "to be their pastor," was among Orientals an ordinary description of a king. Our Lord takes the name to Himself. He is the good Shepherd. St. Peter's rule is also according to this passage of St. John a supreme rule. From a Christian ruler, especially an ecclesiastical ruler, there is required above all things devotedness to the service of his master. The higher the authority the greater must be the devotedness. So St. Peter is gently reminded that he must love his Lord "more than these," *i.e.*, more than the other apostles standing by and, if more than these, certainly more than any besides. Thus St. John confirms our interpretation of St. Matthew, by pointing out St. Peter to us as exalted to the post of

Supreme Ruler over the Christian Church. The two texts are all in the direction of Catholic doctrine.

Against so plain an interpretation what have Anglicans to say? We need not trouble to combat those who claim that not Peter, but either Faith or Christ, is the rock referred to. It is true that some of the Fathers can be quoted in support of such expositions. But in thus expounding, these Fathers have no intention of denying that the text asserted St. Peter's pre-eminence. They differed from the rest merely as to the manner in which this pre-eminence was asserted by the words. It was a discussion about grammar, not theology. Those who took the rock to be faith, meant, not Faith in the abstract, but St. Peter's faith; and they understood his faith to be declared the foundation of the Church in the sense in which a victory is said to be due to the general's skill, instead of to the general himself. It is a mere grammatical figure. The few who took the rock to be Christ, still hold the name Peter, in the assertion "Thou art Peter," to imply that he was a foundation intermediate between Christ and the Church. Moreover none are against us as to the signification of the promise of the Keys and of the power to bind and loose. When we have added that no scholar would any longer hesitate to pronounce the exposition which understands the rock of Peter's person to be the only exposition tenable, it will be seen that no successful escape from the Catholic argument can be obtained by this path. Dean Alford (*in loc.*) says against those who still try to maintain the other theories: "Let us keep to the straightforward sense of Scripture, however that sense may have been misused by Rome:" which is an acknowledgment that up to this point Rome's sense is the only straightforward sense. Nor is it an acknowledgment which reflects upon the ancient Fathers who thought otherwise. We have gained a clearer perception of linguistic processes since their days.

In what then lay the fulfilment, if not in the supremacy of this apostle over the Church, as Catholics understand it? I would here warn the reader to exact a satisfactory answer to this question, and not allow himself to be drawn off to other points till he has received it. Anglican controversialists, having really nothing satisfactory to answer, usually confine themselves to a negative course and amass texts in large quantities from other parts of Scripture which they consider incompatible with the supremacy claimed for the apostle. Under the cover of the dust raised they hope to be allowed to substitute some sort of off-hand exposition which would otherwise have no chance of acceptance. Catholics have really no difficulty in reconciling these other texts with the asserted supremacy, provided time and opportunity be given; but they rightly insist that this extraneous matter should not be used as a blind to withdraw from careful attention the exposition of the text of St. Matthew. This text stands out in the Gospels as one of fundamental importance. Its predictions must then have had a fulfilment correspondingly striking. Where is it?

The answer which finds most favour maintains the reference to be to the ingathering into the Church of the first fruits of the Jews and of the Gentiles. "The fulfilment of the prediction is to be found in the fact that St. Peter was the chosen agent in laying the foundation of the Christian Church both among the Jews (Acts ii. 41) and among the Gentiles (Acts x. 44-48: of Acts xv. 7)." The words quoted are those of the *Speaker's Commentary* and are all it can say on the subject. In the absence of any real arguments to bring forward, it sometimes succeeds to assume what you want as self-evident. Had an attempt been made to show that these events correspond to our Lord's language, the theory must have broken down at once. Notice how in the quotation made St. Peter is said to *lay the foundation* of the Christian Church. To lay the foundation is to contribute the commencing act towards the erection of the building, and had our Lord said, "Thou shalt lay the foundation of the Church," the fulfilment suggested might not have been deemed insufficient. But our Lord said, "Thou art the Rock on which I will build My Church." St. Peter is the foundation, not the architect; he is not even called the foundation stone, but the rock of foundation. The relation of the founder to the building is transient. With the completion of the act of founding, the dependence of the building on its founder ceases. The relation of the foundation stones to the building is twofold. They sustain the building, but they are also the stones first laid. As sustaining, their relation to it is permanent; as first laid, they involve the transient act of laying. The relation of a rock to the building is permanent. It is not laid, but presupposed. Had St. Peter then been called the Founder, the reference would have been to a transient act such as that of receiving into the Church the first fruits of the Jews and Gentiles. Had he been called the Foundation the reference might have been, though need not have been, to the apostle as the first member (*i.e.*, one of the first members) of the Church. Since he is called the Rock the reference is manifestly to some permanent relation which he holds towards the Church as the sustainer of its structure. In view of this, the fulfilment proposed by Anglicans is as clearly inadequate, as that proposed by Catholics and expounded above is clearly adequate. The same reasoning leads to the same result when St. Peter's ministry on the two occasions appealed to is compared with the power of the keys and the power to bind and loose. Again the language implies a permanent office not a single act, and is not satisfied by any isolated acts, such as in Acts viii. 21 : x. 28, when the apostle admitted or ejected a disciple or when he made a particular law. If it is replied that these particular acts are only cited as instances in illustration of a power which he possessed permanently and could exercise as occasion needed, we assent readily. But the admission is fatal. It concedes all that Catholics ascribe to St. Peter's person and supplies the premisses from which the supremacy of his successors can be deduced with certainty, as we hope to show later.

At other times Anglicans grant that by St. Matt. xvi. 13–20 (together with St. John xxi. 13–20) St. Peter is appointed a ruler over the Church, but add that by St. Matt. xviii. 18 the same office was conferred upon the other apostles: whence they deduce that it involved no personal exaltation of St. Peter over his brethren. In confirmation they quote certain of the Fathers as having taught this. Before going further we may advantageously pit these two Anglican expositions against one another. We may cite the supporters of the first as acknowledging that the promise is personal to St. Peter and meant to elevate him above the rest. We may cite the supporters of the second as acknowledging that what is promised is the permanent office of a ruler and not any transient achievement such as the reception into the Christian Church of its first members. Out of these two acknowledgments when combined the Catholic interpretation results. But let us examine this second theory. And first as to the support it claims from the Fathers. The theory includes a statement and a deduction drawn from it—a statement that the self-same office was given likewise to the other apostles, a deduction that therefore St. Peter had no prerogative. It is conceded that certain Fathers, Origen, St. Cyprian, St. Jerome and others support the statement. But none of them made the deduction. On the contrary they all take care to point out that the equality was not absolute. Like Peter, they tell us, the rest were all made rulers, but not supreme rulers. Thus St. Jerome, "The strength of the Church is settled equally upon them (on the apostles): yet for this reason one is chosen out of the twelve, that a Head being appointed, the occasion of schism might be removed."* The principle by which the Fathers are justified in repudiating the deduction, is stated clearly by Bossuet—"Power given to several carries its restriction in its division, whilst power given to one alone, and over all, and without exception, carries with it plenitude, and, not having to be divided with any other it has no bounds save those which its terms convey."†

In case the reader untrained to exegesis should find this principle too abstract to be intelligible, he may consider its form in the concrete by paraphrasing the words of St. Matthew as they would have to be paraphrased were it true that they conferred on St. Peter no pre-eminence over his fellow-disciples. "Blessed art thou, Simon, inasmuch as thou hast learnt by revelation from My Father, and hast openly confessed that I am the Christ, the Son of the Living God. And I say unto thee: Thou art the man whom I have called Peter. I have not made thee, and do not

* *Against Jovinian*, Bk. 1. n. 26. p. 45.
† Sermon on the *Unity of the Church*.

intend to make thee, what this name signifies, at least not exclusively. For if I build My Church upon anything besides Myself, it shall be either upon My apostles generally, or upon true faith in My Eternal Deity. In no case, most blessed Simon, art thou to have any special function or privilege in the matter. For if I build upon the body of the apostles, as upon one rock, thou shalt be only the twelfth part of it: if I build upon them as upon twelve separate rocks, thou shalt be only one of the twelve: and if I build upon the true faith, then every one of My disciples shall be, equally with thyself, the rock upon which My Church shall stand. But to *thee* will I give the keys, the emblem of the supreme ruler's power. Yet again, thou shalt not be the only supreme ruler. These others shall also be supreme rulers as well as thyself, in the one kingdom that I will found on earth. And thou shalt have unlimited judicial and legislative power in My kingdom and all thy laws, all thy orders, all thy judgments shall be ratified by Me in heaven. But I do not, and will not, give 'the faintest intimation that to thy chair there shall be accorded any special pre-eminence of authority or jurisdiction.' The thrones of thy fellow apostles shall be set as high as thine. There shall be no distinction or difference of rank among you. To conclude: though every word of this My solemn congratulation is addressed to thee personally, and personally to thee alone, I would have no one think that aught in it applies especially to thee, except the assertion that thy name is Peter. Blessed art thou, Simon Bar-Jona." The quotation is borrowed from a recent writer. No comment is needed to bring out its force. I trust the reader will now allow me to conclude that St. Peter was really appointed by our Lord to the Supreme Headship of the Church. In another paper it will be shown that the transmission of the Headship to his successors is also deducible from the words of St. Matthew.

III. Papal Supremacy—Can it be proved from the Bible?

In the last chapter it has been shown that the only reasonable interpretation of the impressive words—

"Thou art Peter," etc. (St. Matt. xvi. 13-20), is that which understands them to promise to this apostle the office of supreme visible ruler over the Church. This conclusion is our present starting-point. We have now to carry on the exposition and discover whether the promise was limited to the apostle alone, or included a line of successors who should govern the Church after his death. Anglicans answer very decidedly that St. Peter alone is the recipient of the gift. "The promise is given to St. Peter individually as the person who, by divine revelation, had uttered his confession. Nothing is said or intimated concerning any successor in such an office. With Bengel... we may fairly say, 'Quid hæc ad Romam,' 'what has this to do with Rome?'" (*Speaker's Commentary* on St. Matt. xvi. 13-20). I hope to convince the reader that it has a great deal to do with Rome.

I begin with observing that if the office was not to pass on to successors, it is quite inexplicable why it was conferred on St. Peter. If St. Peter was really made supreme ruler of the Church (and that he was has been clearly demonstrated), the Church must have required a ruler of this kind. Our Lord did not confer empty dignities. The idea which He sought to inculcate upon His apostles was that the ruler was for the people, not the people for the ruler (St. Mark x. 42-45). What the service required of a supreme ruler was, we have been assured by St. Jerome among others—"One is chosen out of the twelve, that a head being appointed, the occasion of schism might be removed"—and what the relation between a supreme headship and the prevention of schism is, has been explained in the first chapter "Can you have Unity without it?" Bearing these considerations in mind, we cannot fail to perceive that a supreme ruler has been much more necessary to the Church since the age of the apostles passed away than he was while that age lasted. The apostles from the time of the Resurrection were men of like mind, confirmed in faith and confirmed in grace. They could be trusted to work together in the great cause committed to their charge. In what an amicable way they were prone to settle any differences of opinion which might rise we can read from the Acts of the Apostles (xv. 6-29: xxi. 20-26). There was no danger lest such men should part off and form themselves into the leaders of distinct and warring sects. To the faithful their attitude was that of a single united whole, adherence to which or separation from which involved the possession or forfeiture of Christian status. In the succeeding generations this happy condition of things no longer continued. The bishops and clergy were not all like the apostles. It was possible, it often happened, that one or more of their number raised the standard of schism and sought to draw away adherents from Catholic Unity. It was then that the Primacy became of vital importance, to make it clear which of the opposing sides was in schism, which faithful to its allegiance. If then the appointment to the office of Supreme Ruler was confined to St. Peter's person and was not intended to pass on, it was given for the time when it was less needed, but withheld for the ages when it would be altogether indispensable.

Still there is nothing in the text about successors. The gift is in reward for the confession that had just been made and is confined to the person who made it. So runs the objection. The answer may be introduced thus. Had our Lord intended to confer an office which should be transmitted to a line of successors after the manner claimed by Catholics, the words actually found in the text would have been a suitable vehicle for His thoughts. The successors could most appropriately be viewed as constituting along with St. Peter a single moral personality, inasmuch as the apostle was to live on in them through their inheritance of his prerogatives and their prosecution of his work. When St. Peter Chrysologus (A.D. 440), writing to Eutyches and referring to the Pope of the day says, "We exhort you, honoured brother, that in all things you obediently attend to those things which have been written by the most blessed Pope (Leo) of the city of Rome, because *blessed Peter, who lives and presides in his own See, gives to those who seek, the true faith;*" * when shortly afterwards the Fathers of the Council of Chalcedon on listening to the letter of the same Pope Leo exclaimed, "*Peter has spoken by Leo;*"† this phraseology is

---

* *Letter to Eutyches.*   † Labbe's *Councils*, T. iv. p. 1235.

exemplified, and it sounds quite naturally to our ears. Whence it appears that there would have been nothing repugnant to the nature of language, if our Lord intending to confer a Primacy destined to last through all time had chosen to speak of it as conferred upon St. Peter without express mention of others, because under the name of St. Peter he wished to denote, not the Peter who was after a few years to shed his blood for the faith commended, but the Peter who should live on through the ages in the long line of heirs to his name and prerogatives. Our Lord could have meant this. But if so, we are entitled to infer that He did mean it; since it has been shown that it is not only a meaning of which the words are susceptible, but the only meaning which does not involve the absurd supposition that the office was given for the time when it was less wanted, but withheld for the time when it was indispensable. At the same time it is not necessary to suppose that the full force of the words was fathomed by him to whom they were addressed. As yet it may not have been realized that generations must come and go between the first and the second advent. As yet the Resurrection had not taken place. As yet the "minds of the apostles had not been opened so as to understand the Scriptures." Later, during the forty days of the first Eastertide, many a private instruction may have been added, and to all likelihood was added, to interpret what the hearers had found obscure in the promise, and to indicate the manner in which the establishment of the Primacy should be carried into execution. These instructions did not however require to be recorded. The simple grandeur of the words of promise unaccompanied by the prosaic details was more in keeping with the austerity of the Gospel style, and more calculated to impress the reader, who, with the light of the fulfilment to aid him, is able to interpret what to the apostles, bereft of this light, would have been obscure without the added instructions.

The Primacy of St. Peter descends to his successors. Who are the successors? When once it has been demonstrated that they exist, there can be no further question where they are to be found. There is but one set of claimants in the field; an uninterrupted line going back to the apostolic age, whose oft-repeated claim was responded to with invariable acknowledgment by the Fathers of the earlier centuries, and through all ages by the members of the only communion which has any pretentions to be exclusively regarded as the world-wide Church of Jesus Christ. I have said that the Fathers acknowledged the Primacy of the Roman Pontiff. Those who have not examined for themselves can have no idea how numerous are the passages which can be collected to substantiate this statement. Many have been collected by Catholic writers, for instance by the Hon. Colin Lindsay in his *Evidence for the Papacy*, and in a more compendious form by Mr. Allnatt in his *Cathedra Petri*. As the limits of a tract do not permit of an array of passages being presented now, it must suffice to appeal to the two quotations made above, one of which has peculiar value as coming from the Fathers of the Fourth General Council (A.D. 451), that of Chalcedon, whose authority Anglicans profess to recognise. As, however, the Third General Council, that of Ephesus, which likewise has to be acknowledged by supporters of the Three Branch Theory, yields a passage of a similar kind, it shall be cited. In this Council, Philip, presbyter and legate of the Apostolic See when about to depose Nestorius, says: "No one doubts, nay it is known to all ages, that the holy and most blessed Peter, the prince and head of the apostles, who is both the pillar of the faith and the foundation of the Catholic Church, received from our Lord Jesus Christ, the Saviour and Redeemer of the human race, the Keys of the Kingdom, and the power to loose and to bind sins was given to him. And he lives to this day and for ever in his successors, and passes sentence. His lawful successor therefore who holds his place, our holy and most Blessed Pope Celestine, &c."* These words were used in the open Council amidst the approbation of all, at the solemn moment when the Council led by the legates was proceeding to depose Nestorius; and they were uttered as exhibiting the authorization which justified the sentence to be passed. What could be more decisive?

---

* Labbe's *Councils*, iii. p. 1194.

Anglicans sometimes venture to contest the historical fact of St. Peter's relation to the See of Rome. In the light of the argument just used, such an objection is at once convicted of frivolousness. Even were there a complete absence of direct evidence of St. Peter's sojourn in Rome, overwhelming evidence of an indirect kind is involved in the universal recognition of the Roman Bishops as his successors, which has existed from the second century downwards. This by itself would be quite sufficient. It cannot be expected that everything which has happened should be preserved in the written record of the very age to which it belongs, especially when the written records of that age are most scanty. Still it is not admitted that convincing direct evidence cannot be supplied. Canon Robertson of Canterbury, who was formerly Professor of Ecclesiastical History at King's College, London, says in his History of the Church: "It is not so much a spirit of sound criticism as religious prejudice, which has led some Protestants to deny that the apostle (St. Peter) was ever at Rome, where all *ancient testimony* represents him to have suffered together with St. Paul in the reign of Nero" (Vol. I, p. 4, ed. 1875). Canon Robertson no doubt testifies here only to the evidence for the presence of St. Peter in the city of Rome, not of his having been bishop of its Church. But the evidence in favour of St. Peter's Roman episcopate is just as strong as that in favour of his Roman visit. In both cases it is only a religious prejudice which prevents recognition of a fact to which all ancient testimony points.

IV. Papal Infallibility—What does it mean?

This is an age fed on newspapers. It is to newspapers that most of us largely, and many of us entirely, look for information and for opinions. On the other hand the information and the opinions supplied from this source are given to be crude, inaccurate, and often false. Journalists are men in a hurry. They are obliged to form opinions on the spur of the moment as the hour of publication will not wait, and in consequence they get into the habit of making rash guesses and judging from insufficient evidence. One of the subjects which comes in this way to be much talked of and little understood is Papal Infallibility. The word is on everybody's lips. Everybody is intensely shocked that the Pope should make so outrageous a claim. Meanwhile how many are there who could tell you what the claim is, how many are there who even understand the meaning of the word?

What is Infallibility? Many seem to think it means sinlessness. To assert that the Pope is infallible is, according to them, to assert that he never sins, and never can sin. Then they ask, does not the Bible teach that all have sinned, that, "there is none that doeth right, no not one" (Rom. iii 12)? They go further and ask, what about the bad Popes, and they speak as though moral depravity were an admitted characteristic of that illustrious line. Here they greatly exaggerate. There have indeed been Popes, whose histories can only be read with sorrow. They have been to the Apostolic See what Judas was among the Apostles. Nor is this wonderful, seeing how often ambitious princes and nobles have endeavoured under threat of arms to impose their worldly-minded candidates on the electors. It is a bad thing for the Church when the State succeeds in over-ruling its counsels. Still the wonder is, not that there have been so many bad Popes, but that there have been so few. Since St. Peter, that is during eighteen centuries and a half, there have been over two hundred and fifty Pontiffs; and since the Conquest, that is during eight centuries, there have been thirty-five Sovereigns of England. Yet if you compare together the two lists, you will find more bad kings during the shorter period than you will find bad Popes during the longer. In fact only four or five Popes have been in any way proved to have been bad. As a whole, the line of Popes has been a line of men quite remarkable for personal holiness. However, Infallibility has nothing to do with holiness of life. When the Pope is said to be infallible, the meaning is, not that he cannot do what is wrong, but that he cannot teach what is false. The word *infallible* means incapable of deceiving or being deceived.

But is it conceivable that God should grant so high a gift as this of immunity from error in faith to men whose lives are sinful? Yes, it is, and for this reason. The gift is granted to them, not for their own personal advantage, but for the advantage of the Church at large. If the object of Infallibility were the personal benefit of the Popes, it is quite true that God would hardly grant it to men of evil life. But since it is given for the sake of the Church, in order that the faithful throughout the world may always be preserved in the truth, it is quite in accordance with the analogies of God's merciful Providence that it should not be withheld even from the worst of sinners, when once he had been duly elected to the Pontificate. The case is exactly similar to that of the administration of the Sacraments. Baptism and Holy Communion are valid Sacraments and profitable to the receiver when duly administered, even if the minister should unfortunately be guilty in the eyes of God of the most grievous sins. Anglicans admit this as much as Catholics.

Since infallibility is immunity from error in doctrine, it is an attribute of the Popes as *teachers*, not as *rulers*. Catholics do indeed believe that God watches over the supreme government of the Church with a very special providence, and they are always loth to admit injustice or even unwisdom in Papal rule. In fact they are sure that in its general character this rule is both wise and holy. They are sure also that laws imposed upon the entire Church cannot be such as it would be wrong to obey. Still it is not claimed that the Popes may not at times impose commands neither wise nor even just. It is even allowed that their commands may at times, though rarely, be clearly wrong : in which case it would be a matter of conscience to refuse obedience. Bishop Grosseteste refused to obey the Pope's order to admit to a benefice in his diocese a certain candidate appointed by the Pope. He said the candidate was unfit and his conscience would not allow him to institute. Taking the facts to be as Grosseteste affirmed, Catholics would say now, just as much as ever before, that he was right to resist. The Pope himself acknowledged as much when remonstrated with. Many similar instances could be cited. One of recent occurrence, when there was a question not of right or wrong but of desirability, may be mentioned. When the German Catholics showed some reluctance to accept the present Pope's recommendation, and vote in favour of Prince Bismarck's Army Bill, the *Times* expressed sarcastic surprise that such faithful sons of the Church should demur to the orders of their Infallible Pope. In reality there was no order, only a suggestion. But even had there been an order, and it had referred to matters more strictly ecclesiastical, the German Catholics might still have felt it to be inadvisable without any disloyalty to the dogma of Infallibility. The question was one of government, not of teaching. Of course it does not follow that they could without disloyalty disobey, or without disloyalty be over prone to impute imprudence to the injunctions of authority. Nothing however could have been more loyal than their actual conduct.

Even in regard to teaching there are restrictions to be applied to the general description with which we have hitherto been contented, before an exact notion of the nature of Infallibility can be obtained. *First*, it refers only to teaching concerning Faith and Morals, it does not refer to teaching concerning secular subjects disconnected with these. The Pope is not infallible on Mathematics and Physics. If Physics and Theology are both involved in the determination of a controversy the case is different. The Theology would be within the Pope's competence and might fall under his infallibility. Indirectly this would strike any inconsistent views on Physics, but not directly. *Secondly*, the Pope is not always infallible even in regard to Faith and Morals; but only when he is speaking officially. Some of the Popes, Benedict XIV, for instance, have been also theological writers. Infallibility does not attach to their published writings, still less does it attach to their private conversations. In neither of these cases are they speaking officially. *Thirdly*, the Vatican Council does not claim infallibility even for all their official teaching: only for their *ex cathedrâ* teaching. The phrase *ex cathedrâ* means literally "from the Chair" (*i.e.* of Truth) and according to the same Vatican definition, the Pope teaches from this Chair "when, discharging his office of Pastor and Teacher of *all Christians*, in virtue of his supreme Apostolic authority, he defines a doctrine concerning faith and morals as to be held by the *whole Church.*" Thus he must be addressing, not some individual person nor some particular portion of the Church, but the entire Church. He must be addressing them not anywise, but with the *intention* of using his supreme authority to oblige them to render assent to his definition. And of course he must make it manifest to them that he has this intention: otherwise the corresponding obligation to believe does not arise.

When these conditions are borne in mind, it is seen that almost all the objections usually urged in disproof of Papal Infallibility are irrelevant. Take for instance the one which is most relied upon, that based on the declaration extorted from Galileo who was bidden by the Inquisition to affirm that "the sun goes round the earth." This was an order imposed, not on the whole Church, but on a single man. It was imposed by a Congregation of Cardinals, not by the Pope: or if it be said that the Pope was much mixed up in the matter and lent his entire sanction to the orders given to Galileo, at all events he neither gave his name to the written documents nor was acting in virtue of his supreme apostolic authority as the teacher of all Christians. Infallibility is a great responsibility. Although knowing well that his deliberations are being overruled by God, and that it is to this over-ruling providence not to the perspicacity of his own intellectual powers that the infallibility of the conclusion will be primarily due, still the Pope is bound to use his natural powers to the best of his ability and under a profound sense of responsibility, if he wishes to proceed to a definition of faith. Hence these definitions are only issued after long-continued examinations, consultations and discussions, after much prayer and consideration. They are consequently rare. Now it is obvious that the Pope may often have to act under circumstances which do not require infallibility to be staked upon their issue. He will then give his orders as Pope, but not in virtue of his supreme apostolical authority. So was it in the case of Galileo. Urban VIII acted as Pope, but not as supreme teacher. The documentary evidence bears out this statement. It offers no ground for imputing to Pope Urban an intention to draw upon his infallibility—quite the contrary. In a similar manner St. Peter's submission to the rebuke of St. Paul yields no ground of attack against this dogma. St. Peter was not addressing the whole Church; he was not teaching at all. His conduct was reprehended: and it was reprehended as being inconsistent with his own undoubted teaching.

V. Papal Infallibility—Is it according to Reason?

On a recent occasion an Anglican Bishop declared it to be evident that "the dogma of Papal Infallibility is the stultification of reason." Such a phrase to knock down an opponent with is all that is required by the unthinking majority. It is admirably adapted for platform and newspaper use, and no doubt was taken down for that purpose with grateful pencils by the listeners. But fortunately there are some who refuse to be led by phrases until they have submitted them to the test of careful examination. It is to readers of this class that the present paper is addressed.

Is Papal Supremacy then the stultification of human reason? A law which assured children that they needed no instructors, and that their highest duty was to follow their own lights would be a stultification of reason; on the other hand a law to compel youth with its want of knowledge and its infirmity of judgment to sit at the feet of age and experience is eminently according to reason. Which of these does the dogma of Papal Infallibility most resemble? Does it set up an incompetent teacher over those who need none, or does it supply with a competent teacher those who without one would be all astray? We see now that the question resolves itself into these two. Does the world need a trustworthy teacher? and does the doctrine of Papal Infallibility supply it with one in a suitable manner?

To the first question there can hardly be a doubt what answer should be rendered. There are indeed persons who think religious truth is a matter of infinitely small importance. "No matter what you believe as long as you do right" they tell you. If truth were really of no consequence, a trustworthy teacher would be a superfluity. But the maxim just given comes to this: "It does not matter whether you know the way as long as you go by it." If you do not know the way, how can you go by it? Evidently our Blessed Lord thought truth to be of importance. "I came to bear witness to the truth," He tells us (St. John xviii. 37). If truth were of no consequence, it is not conceivable that He should have come down from heaven and have taken flesh in order to become our instructor and even to seal His testimony with His Blood. Revealed Truth therefore is of importance, of the highest importance. How then are we to attain to it? In the earlier days of Protestantism a method was proposed which sounds simple enough. All that is necessary is written down in the Bible. Read this reverently and with prayer, and you will find it. But those who try it soon find out that the Bible, although it "does one good to read it," is a very hard book to understand. Those who go to it in this manner for doctrines, relying on their own private judgment for its interpretation, are found to return with results altogether inconsistent and even opposite. Thus it is clear to sensible persons that if the Bible is to be of any use a trustworthy teacher is needed to explain it.

Our first question above propounded is now answered. But where is the teacher to be found? It is natural first to think of ministers of religion. Every denomination, or nearly every denomination, of Christians has found it necessary to appoint ministers to conduct its services and preside over the adminstration of its religious organization. Such ministers being men who have studied divinity, it might seem that one could consult them with confidence. But here again the same difficulty recurs. These ministers do not agree among themselves. Go and ask Mr. Johnston the Vicar and Mr. Thompson the Dissenting minister, for instance, what is the right means of obtaining forgiveness of sins; and although each will claim that the instruction which he gives you is in accordance with the teaching of the Bible, their answers will be different and even opposite. Both cannot be right. Both cannot be trustworthy teachers. Is either of them? and if so by what mark is he to be known as such? Perhaps the Anglican Vicar will tell you that the mark is membership of the Church, that Mr. Thompson being a Dissenter is in schism, that it is not surprising that schismatic ministers should teach you wrong, that if you want sound teaching you must seek it from the ministers of the Church, which goes back to the times of the apostles. Of course by "the Church" he means his so-called Church of England, though whether this institution has any ground for claiming descent from the apostles is again a matter of dispute. If you take the Vicar's advice it will not extricate you from your perplexity. The Vicar of High Hampton says you must get absolution from an episcopally ordained priest: the Vicar of Low Hampton repels this suggestion with indignation and directs you to pray for saving faith: the Vicar of Broad Hampton pooh-poohs the recommendations of both his brethren and assures you nothing more is required than to strive in future to live according to the commandments. The Vicar of High Hampton lights candles on his altar and bids you fall down in solemn adoration before Christ present in the Sacrament: the Vicar of Low Hampton declares this to be rank idolatry: while the Vicar of Broad Hampton takes a middle course and pronounces it all to be a quarrel about metaphysical subtleties. If now you enter into yourself and ask how comes it that these gentlemen disagree so much, the answer is plain. Each goes by his own judgment as exercised on the text of Holy Scripture and perhaps on the literature of the first Christian centuries. But man's judgment is essentially fallible and the fallibility of his judgments is revealed in the multitudinous differences of opinion, which, when the subject is at all difficult, commend themselves to different minds. These gentlemen are all fallible, and convicted of fallibility by their differences of view. None of them is fit to be my guide. On the teaching of none of them can I reasonably rely. So far I seem to have three times discovered stultification of the reason in the proposals submitted for my acceptance. It is stultification of reason to regard creed as unimportant, whereas it is the only means of guiding conduct. It is stultification of reason to set myself up as a trustworthy interpreter of the Bible. It is stultification of reason to submit myself blindly to teachers who reveal their untrustworthiness by their disagreements.

What is it then which my reason really demands? Evidently a teacher set up by God and not by man; one rendered absolutely trustworthy, not because he is naturally more wise or more learned than other men, but because he is protected from falling into error when he teaches the Church, by the Holy Spirit of God which watches over him. If there is such an one in the world the need which we all feel to know with accuracy and certainty what our Lord has bidden us to believe and what He has bidden us to do, is at once supplied after a manner suitable to our nature and easy of application. The infallible teacher is placed at the head of a vast body of other teachers appointed under him in various grades. These subordinate teachers need not themselves be infallible. All required is that they shall teach in conformity with their infallible Head, and this is sufficiently secured by the solicitude with which the latter watches over them, and with which he corrects and if necessary displaces any whom his watchful eye detects as departing from the doctrine which he himself, under the guidance of the Divine Spirit, knows to be alone revealed. Notice that the effect of this simple and natural arrangement will be to provide the faithful everywhere with living teachers upon whom they can rely, and at the same time to mark these with a character by which they can be securely distinguished from the teachers who go only by their own lights. This character will consist in the complete agreement among themselves which the teachers in communion with the infallible Head exhibit. They will all teach alike. It is a character the nature of which the least instructed can appreciate. It requires no great learning to know that disagreement is the mark of error and uncertainty: agreement on an extensive scale the mark of truth securely possessed. We are dealing in this paper with a scheme in the abstract, not with its concrete realization in the bishops and priests who recognise the Infallibility of the Pope. Still the concrete realization may be suitably appealed to as an illustration of the explanation given. You may indeed be told by

Anglicans that Catholic priests disagree among themselves as much as anybody else. Still if instead of listening to such Anglicans you make the experiment yourself, you will find that they have misinformed you. Ask any Catholic priest you like what is the appointed means of obtaining the forgiveness of sins, and they will tell you Baptism for those who have not received it; and for the baptized Priestly Absolution. Ask a friend in Spain or America, or China, to make the same inquiry there; the answer will be the same. Why? Because a priest who should persist in teaching that Priestly Absolution was not of divine appointment would at once be removed by his bishop: as in like manner a bishop who presumed to depart from this doctrine of the Church would be removed by the Pope. As with this one doctrine, so with the whole range of doctrines by which the Christian life is regulated. It is quite true that there are questions concerning which you will find differences of opinion even among the Catholic clergy. But this, so far from destroying the value of the agreement where it lies, stamps it with the further confirmation of contrast. Where the Pope speaks, there they all speak with him and hence agree; where he has not spoken, and they have only their own judgment to go by, they relapse into the condition of other men and disagree. However the area of settled questions is wide, and covers all matters of practical importance. Thus whatever disagreement exist in reference to ulterior points is innocuous. Herein lies the difference between the domestic controversies of Catholics and of Protestants. The former, turning only on minor and mostly purely speculative points, are consistent with uniformity in Christian practice; the latter ranging as they do over the entire field of revealed truth produce the greatest perplexity among the people, who are rendered quite unable to shape their course of conduct in essential matters.

This is what is meant by Papal Infallibility. Surely it sounds most reasonable; and yet we are told that such a doctrine is the stultification of reason. In what does the stultification consist? Certainly not in placing a teacher over those who need none; for it has been shown that this is just what men do need. Certainly not in establishing a system which cannot work: for it has been shown how easily and naturally it works. Certainly not in assigning a teacher incompetent for the task: since the teacher assigned is not the Pope as a mere man, but the Pope under the special guidance of the Holy Spirit, so that the real teacher is God. Is it foolish to believe that God can so overrule the reasonings of a human mind as to prevent it from falling into error? This ought not at any rate to be accounted foolish by Anglicans who believe in the Infallibility of General Councils. If God can overrule the deliberations of a Council, that is, of a number of men, still more can he overrule the deliberations of a single man. Nor ought it to be accounted foolish by any of those who believe in the Inspiration of Holy Scripture. Inspiration involves a still more far-reaching interposition on the part God than is required for Infallibility. Is Infallibility too great a burden for a man to bear, so that it is absurd to suppose that God would, even if He could, impose it? If Infallibility attended the Popes in their every utterance, even in those bearing on secular matters and on the daily intercourse of life, perhaps it might lift them too much out of the natural order and above the conditions under which alone human probation is possible. But there is no such impropriety in an Infallibility which is confined to a limited class of official utterances, and this is all which the Vatican Council has claimed for the Popes. It does not appear in what other respect stultification of the reason can be discovered in the dogma, and at all events we may wait till Anglicans have indicated it.

VI. Papal Infallibility—Has it been always believed?

By the Infallibility of the Pope, Catholics mean that immunity from error in his sacred teaching which they claim for the Head of their Church. Its nature and significance has been expounded in the last two chapters, and a strong presumption thereby established for the genuineness of the claim. It remains to convert the presumption into proof. As a principal point relied upon by opponents of the claim is its supposed novelty, while on the other hand, proof of its genuineness is largely mixed up with proof of its antiquity, it will be desirable to consider these two points simultaneously. Is the claim ancient, and is it original; that is, based on a real grant made by our Blessed Lord? Before commencing we must endeavour to understand our terms. The charge of novelty rests upon an equivocation which must be exposed. The doctrine is ancient, but its formal definition by an Œcumenical Council is recent, having taken place at the Vatican Council in 1870, as everybody knows. There is no inconsistency between these two statements. It is not by definition alone that the Church teaches. She teaches by her daily instruction, given in sermons, books, catechisms, services, devotions, &c., which is carried on under her watchful eye and virtual approval; as also under a stimulus and express direction which she has imparted. Definitions are of the nature of judicial decisions. They presuppose a controversy as to what the Church's teaching really is, and their purpose is to terminate the question by a clear declaration calculated to remove the doubt or obscurity, rational or irrational, out of which the controversy grew. If there were no controversies there would be no definitions. To conclude that the teaching of a certain doctrine is new, because the definition which declares it to be a genuine portion of revelation is recent, is as absurd as it would be absurd to conclude that, because a judge's decision on a point of law is recent, the law which it declares is also new.

If we put this same matter in another way, it will serve the better to illustrate the position. The controversy precedent to the definition of Infallibility, although it was ultimately a controversy about the truth of the dogma, was immediately one about its age. Was it novel and therefore false, or was it old and therefore true? The Vatican definition declared it to be old. "We, *adhering faithfully to the tradition handed down from the commencement of the Christian faith* . . . teach and define it to be a dogma of divine revelation that the Roman Pontiff, when he speaks *ex cathedrâ*, is through the Divine assistance assured to him in Blessed Peter, possessed of that Infallibility, etc." (Chap. iv.) But, it is urged, before the Vatican Council Infallibility could be denied without danger of anathema, whereas, according to the Catholics, a similar denial at the present time would certainly incur that penalty. This is true, but it does not show that previously the doctrine was in fact no part of the Church's teaching: it only shows that in the absence of a judicial decision, that is of a definition, it was possible conscientiously to doubt whether the doctrine was part of her teaching. After the definition, such a doubt can no longer remain in the mind of a loyal Catholic; refusal to accept the dogma is therefore without excuse.

There is still another precaution to be observed before the true value of the historical evidence for the antiquity of the doctrine can be appreciated. Although we claim that the doctrine is old, we are well aware that its formulation as a theological proposition and its designation by this particular name of Infallibility does not go back many centuries. This kind of formulation is the result of the scientific study to which controversy more than anything else gives birth. But under simpler modes of expression essentially the same doctrine was practically held and acted upon from the first. The forms under which it is found are such as these: (1) That the Pope is the Supreme Teacher of the Catholic Church. (2) That no one can reject his teaching without sin and without cutting himself off from the communion of the faithful. (3) That in the See of Rome the sacred doctrine has ever been preserved immaculate. (4) That this prerogative is derived from St. Peter whose own faith was confirmed in order that he might confirm the faith of others. Of these four propositions the third is the assertion of infallibility; the first and second state the purpose for which it is required, the premises from which it follows as a corollary: the fourth traces it to the origin whence it sprang. If then we find these same propositions asserted in early times by representative men before the face of the whole Church without encountering contradiction, we have all that is needful, although the technical name of Infallibility is one not then devised.

Has it always been believed? 31

When at last we turn to ecclesiastical history, we discover that it is not the doctrine of Papal Infallibility, but the denial of this doctrine which is wanting in the necessary antiquity. According to the theory of those Catholics who denied the Pope to be infallible, the organ of Infallibility is a General Council without the Pope, or at all events only a General Council with the Pope. Until the fifteenth century no trace of such a theory can be discovered. But at that time an antipope had been set up against the true Pope, and it was not easy to get at the facts so as to ascertain which of them had been properly elected. This caused a great deal of perplexity; and it occurred to a few venturesome persons to start the theory that a Council of the Church as representing the whole Church was superior to the Pope who was but a part of it, so that a Council of this sort could properly sit in judgment on the rival candidates. The theory was at once caught up by courtier ecclesiastics, who saw how readily it could be turned to the advantage of the French sovereigns in their attack upon the liberties of the Church. It was therefore fostered, particularly in France, and sought, though in vain, admission among the legitimate decrees of the Council of Constance. It lived on till the Vatican Council.

While the first appearance of the opposition is discoverable in the fourteenth century, the traces of belief in Papal Infallibility are discernible all down the course of the previous centuries. We must content ourselves with one or two crucial instances.

To the Second Council of Lyons, an Œcumenical Council held in A.D. 1274, the Greek Emperor, desirous of restoring to unity the Greeks who had formed a schism some four hundred years earlier, sent an embassy to represent him. They made a profession of faith in which occur the following words: "The Holy Roman Church (*i.e.*, the See of Rome) holds the Primacy and princedom over the entire Catholic Church: and truly and humbly acknowledges that she has received it from the Lord Himself in Blessed Peter the prince and head of the apostles, together with the plenitude of power. *And as before the others she is bound to defend the truth of the faith:* so also, *whatever question concerning faith may* *arise, ought to be decided by her judgment,"* &c.,* with much else in recognition of the Primacy. Here we have the substance of propositions 1 and 4 out of those above stated. This act of profession is most valuable, because it was made before an approving assemblage of five hundred bishops, seventy abbots, and one thousand prelates and legates of princes (among whom were the prelates of the old Church of England), by men specially sent to represent the Orientals. Letters of adhesion were brought by these Greek legates in the name of the Emperor, twenty-nine Eastern metropolitans with their respective synods, and many other ecclesiastics. It is thus an irrefragable witness to the faith of the Latin Church two hundred years before the opposing doctrine was heard of, and a witness to the faith of that body of Orientals, which Anglicans dignify with the title of Second Branch of the Church Universal. It is true the Orientals soon fell back, but that is to their own disgrace; the letters of adhesion remain to testify against them.

Two hundred years earlier, the Fourth Council of Constantinople, the Eighth Œcumenical Council, was held (A D. 869). This was just before the Photian schism, which gave rise to the Greek "Branch," was consummated. Pope Hadrian II. sent over a profession of faith with orders that no one should be admitted to sit in the Council without having first subscribed it. The conditions were accepted. All who sat, about a hundred in number and the pick of the Eastern Church for piety of life, attached their signatures. The document runs thus: "The first condition of salvation *(prima salus)* is to hold the right rule of faith and in no way stray from the decrees of the Fathers. And because the sentence of our Lord Jesus Christ Who said 'Thou art Peter,' &c., cannot be passed over, what was there said is proved by the result of events, for in the Apostolic See *religion has ever been preserved immaculate.* By no means wishing *to be separated from the hope and faith of this (See),* and following the decrees of the Fathers, and especially of the holy bishops of the Apostolic See in all things, we anathematize

---

* Labbe's *Councils,* xiv. p. 512.

all heresies. . . . Whence, as we have said, *following the Apostolic See in all things* and professing all its decrees, I trust that I may deserve to be with you *in the one communion* which the *Apostolic See enjoins*, in which is the entire and true solidity of the Christian religion. Promising also that the names of these *who are cut off from the communion of the Catholic Church, that is, who are not consentient with the Apostolic See*, shall not be recited during the Sacred Mysteries."* In this celebrated document we have all the four propositions above given. It is called the Formula of Pope Hormisdas, because three hundred and fifty years earlier (A.D. 519), it was drawn up by that Pope and was subscribed in like manner by the Emperor, the Patriarchs and the Bishops of the East. According to Dr. Döllinger this formula was then signed altogether by about 2500 Eastern Bishops (Hist. of Church, vol. ii. p. 221). Thus we have three most formal declarations testifying to the belief in Papal Infallibility of both East and West. Of these the first has brought us back to the commencement of the sixth century.

Out of the first half of the fifth we may summon St. Peter Chrysologus, the great Bishop of Ravenna, to testify: not because others are wanting, but because of the distinctness of his language. He is writing to Eutyches the Monophysite and says: "*Blessed Peter*, who lives and presides in his own See, *gives the true faith to those who seek it.* For we, in our solicitude for truth and faith, *cannot without the consent of the Roman Church hear causes of faith.*"† This doctrine is exactly the same as that enunciated in the Formula of Hormisdas a hundred years later, and yet it has already an air of antiquity. It is not put forward with hesitation, or as an opinion, but rather as a well-known and generally recognised truth. A few years later the same Eutyches whom St. Peter Chrysologus is addressing was to hear the same doctrine proclaimed loudly by the Council of Chalcedon, when after listening to the letter of Pope Leo which was written in his condemnation all the assembled fathers

---

* Labbe's *Councils*, x. p. 498 and v. p. 586.
† *Letter to Eutyches.*

cried out, "Peter has spoken by Leo." We go back still another century and the great St. Ambrose is our witness, one out of several. The saint's brother, Satyrus, was a bishop of suspect faith, and this is how Ambrose handles him. "He called the bishop to him and not accounting any grace true *which was not of the true faith*, he enquired of him *whether he agreed with the Catholic Bishops, that is with the Roman Church*" (*De Excessu Fratris*). With St. Ambrose then agreement with the Roman Bishop is the appointed test of orthodoxy; the indispensable condition of communion with the Catholic Church. And the tone is still that of antiquity, of long-established recognition, although we are now not three centuries removed from the last of the apostles, and are in the midst of an age which stands out among the rest as being pre-eminently that of those Fathers who have ever been regarded the most authoritative witnesses to primitive tradition.

It is noticeable that in the passages adduced this prerogative of Infallibility is always traced back to St. Peter, and to the classical passage in the sixteenth chapter of St. Matthew's Gospel, whence Catholics derive his authority. From the chapter on the Bible witness to the Supremacy the reader may see how distinctly the first of them (St. Matt. xvi. 16) asserts the Primacy of the Apostle (and his successors). A still more searching examination shows that it is especially in his quality of a teacher that St. Peter is thus regarded. It is his firm faith which is rewarded, the faith by which he was the first to confess the Divinity of his Master. When the reward takes the form of establishing the apostle in strength in order that he may impart it in his turn to the Church, as a rock does to the superstructure, it is most natural to understand the strengthening to be primarily a strengthening of faith. He is a rock to the Church by reason of his faith, inasmuch as its members are established in their own faith by rendering obedient assent to his infallible teaching. This also our Lord Himself, in words free from figure, declares elsewhere; "Simon, Simon, Satan has desired to have *you* (in the plural) that he may sift you as wheat, but I have prayed for *thee* (in the singular) that *thy faith may not fail*, and do thou in thy turn (this is the more probable rendering) *confirm* thy brethren" (St. Luke xxii. 31, 32). This is another text the Fathers frequently refer to and understand in the sense asserted. It is true that some see an allusion to the triple denial shortly to follow. But these are not to be understood as wishing to exclude the more direct reference on which Fathers and Councils more often dwell. Indeed it is most probable there is an allusion to St. Peter's denial, but it is an allusion only, and does not belong to the direct scope of the words, at all events it does not exhaust their meaning. Let those who think otherwise offer some reasonable account of the way in which the Apostle confirmed his brethren.

Conclusion.

The conclusions at which we have arrived may be summed up as follows. The doctrines of Papal Supremacy and Infallibility are neither unreasonable nor extravagant. If they are true, a means has been provided of maintaining the Christian people in the bonds of unity, which is simple and easy of application, and at the same time in harmony with the nature of man. If they are not true, the inevitable result must be what we find it to be in fact wherever the Pope's authority is not acknowledged: indifferentism in place of a common faith, innumerable schisms in place of sacramental intercommunion, religious anarchy in place of ecclesiastical order. There is then the strongest presumption that the system which the two doctrines represent is that which our Lord has established, since otherwise He would have made Himself responsible for all these horrors which good people deplore. This is the first conclusion which has been arrived at.

A second is that the evidence yielded by Scripture and Ecclesiastical History, when interpreted according to the laws of right reason, points exactly in the same direction. It shows that our Lord has ordained what we should have expected Him to ordain. These two things, the presumption and the proof, should be considered together. Through their harmony each adds strength to the other. They are like the strands of a rope which gain strength from being intertwined.

But what about the opposing evidence, an Anglican may exclaim? Is only one side to be heard? Would that Anglicans would always make a point of hearing both sides! Too often they only hear what is said against the Papacy, not what is to be said on its behalf. Under such circumstances it might seem excusable to urge only the latter, leaving the former to take care of itself. There is, however, no desire on the part of Catholics to evade a single one of the difficulties which can be brought against the doctrines and institutions they believe to be divine. On the contrary, there is the greatest desire to deal with them all solidly and thoroughly, so that every impediment may be cleared away from the path of those who are anxious to find the truth. Still one thing at a time, and the examination of the proofs has been found quite sufficient matter for this series of papers. It may be added that the difficulties are far from being as serious as is commonly imagined. A satisfactory answer to very many will at once suggest itself, if the doctrinal explanations which have been given are borne carefully in mind.

THE BIBLE AND THE REFORMATION.

BY C. F. B. ALLNATT.

THERE has long existed amongst Protestants of all denominations a wide-spread delusion, that the "glorious Reformation" in this and other countries was mainly brought about by the printing of the Holy Scriptures in the vernacular, and the copious dissemination of copies of the same amongst the people. No sooner, we are often told, had the laity been put in possession of "an open Bible," than they at once discovered the errors of Popery, and hastened to embrace the true Gospel preached by the Reformers.

Now history tells us a very different tale. As regards our own country, for instance,—for it is with that we are now mainly concerned,—the Presbyterian Lord MACAULAY has observed : "A King, whose character may be best described by saying that he was despotism itself personified, unprincipled ministers, a rapacious aristocracy, a servile Parliament, *such* were the instruments by which England was delivered from the yoke of Rome. The work which had been begun by Henry, the murderer of his wives, was continued by Somerset, the murderer of his brother, and completed by Elizabeth, the murderer of her guest. . . . Of those who had any important share in bringing the Reformation about, Ridley was perhaps the only person who did not consider it as *a mere political job*" (*Essay on Hallam*).

I will not now stop to inquire into the *motives*—whether political or personal—which actuated the leaders of the revolt against the Church: it will be enough to state, in the words of another non-Catholic historian, what were the chief *means* by which their revolutionary work was accomplished. On this point Mr. LECKY says: "With the exception of *Z*uinglius and Socinus [the founder of the Socinian sect], all the most eminent Reformers advocated *persecution;* and in nearly every country where their boasted Reformation triumphed, the result is mainly to be attributed to *coercion*" (*Hist. of Ration. in Europe*, vol. ii. p. 45). This is confirmed by HALLAM, who remarks: "Persecution is the deadly original sin of the Reformed Churches, that which cools every honest man's zeal for their cause, in proportion as his reading becomes more extensive" (*Constit. Hist. of Eng.* vol. i. ch. 3).

It is perfectly true that the royal tyrants named by Macaulay, and those who aided and abetted them in their nefarious designs, endeavoured to give a religious colour and sanction to their doings by the publication of English Bibles, and by hypocritical exhortations to the multitude to read the same for themselves; but it has long been a notorious fact that all these Protestant versions of the Bible literally swarmed with the grossest and most flagrant corruptions—corruptions consisting in the wilful and deliberate mistranslation of various passages of the sacred text, and all directly aimed against those doctrines and practices of the Catholic Church which the "Reformers" were most anxious to uproot. They did give the people "an open Bible," but *what* a Bible! I will now give only the following specimens of it :—

1. We have heard a good deal of late about the "continuity" of the Anglican Establishment with the old Catholic Church of this country. The "Reformers" held no such doctrine. They taught that "the whole of Christendom had been altogether drowned in damnable idolatry for the space of eight hundred years and more" (*Hom. on Peril of Idolatry*, part iii.), and they so abhorred the very name of the "CHURCH," that they expunged it from almost every passage of the New Testament in which it occurs, and substituted in the place of it the word "*congregation !*" Thus, in St. Matt. xvi. 18, instead of "On this rock I will build My *Church*," Tyndall's Bible, Cranmer's Bible, the Geneva Bible, and the Bishops' Bible read : " On this rock I will build My CONGREGATION "! "Tell it unto the *Church*" (St. Matt. xviii. 17) is in the three first of these versions corrupted into, " Tell it unto the CONGREGATION ;"

and the same heretical perversion of course occurs in Ephes. i. 22; ch. v. 23—25; 1 Tim. iii. 15; Heb. xii. 23, and various other passages. In the first English Bible the word "Church" did not once occur! It was not until a considerable number of the English people had been deceived, betrayed, and coerced into abandoning the ancient faith, and formed what might outwardly *resemble* a national Church, that their Protestant rulers ventured to restore the word "Church" to the English Bible!

2. So again, wherever the word "idols," or "idolatry" occurred in the New Testament, the early Protestant translators substituted instead "*images*," and "*image-worship*"—with the intention, of course, of inducing the ignorant people to believe that all images of our Lord and the saints had been forbidden in the Word of God! Where we now read, "Little children, keep yourselves from *idols*" (1 St. John v. 21), there the "open Bibles" of the Reformation had, "Babes, keep yourselves from *images*!"

"Covetousness, which is *idolatry*" (Col. iii. 5), is, in the Bibles of 1534, 1539, 1568, turned into "covetousness, which is *worshipping of images*." "How agreeth the temple of God with *idols*" (2 Cor. vi. 16) reads, in the Bibles of 1534, 1539, 1557, 1562, "How agreeth the temple of God with *images*?"

3. Wherever Apostolic "*Traditions*" were commended in the New Testament, the word was

carefully expunged, and the word "*ordinances*" put in its place; whilst, on the other hand, the word "traditions" was in several instances foisted into the text (as in 1 St. Peter i. 18), where it did not occur in the original Greek, for the purpose of making the very name odious in the eyes of the ignorant Protestant multitude! St. Paul says: "Hold fast the *Traditions* ye have received of us" (2 Thess. ii. 15; iii. 6); but this did not at all suit the doctrine or conduct of Tyndall, Cranmer, and the rest; so, as I have said, they expunged the word in these texts (see also 1 Cor. xi. 2, corrected in the "Revised Version"), though they took care to retain it in those passages of the Gospels in which the *false* "traditions" of the Pharisees were condemned by our Lord.

Protestant writers and lecturers would have us believe that the earlier Bible of WICKLIFFE had been prohibited by the Church authorities of his time simply on account of their general hostility to the Word of God in the vernacular. Nothing could be more contrary to the truth. A better informed Protestant writer, the Rev. E. CUTTS, D.D., in a work published by the Society for Promoting Christian Knowledge, observes:—"There is a good deal of popular misapprehension about the way in which the Bible was regarded in the middle ages. Some people think that it was very little read, even by the clergy; whereas the fact is that the sermons of the mediæval preachers are more full of Scripture quotations and allusions than any sermons in these days; and the writers on other subjects are so full of Scriptural allusion, that it is evident their minds were saturated with Scriptural diction. . . . Another common error is, that the clergy were unwilling that the laity should read the Bible for themselves, and carefully kept it in an unknown tongue, that the people might not be able to read it. The truth is, that most people who could read at all could read Latin, and would certainly prefer to read the authorized Vulgate to any vernacular version. But it is also true that translations into the vernacular were made. . . . We have the authority of Sir Thomas More for saying that 'the whole Bible was, long before Wycliff's days, by virtuous and well-learned men translated into the English tongue, and by good and godly people with devotion and soberness well and reverently read.' . . . Again, on another occasion he says: 'The clergy keep no Bibles from the laity but such translations as be either not yet approved for good, or such as be already reproved for naught (bad), as Wycliffe's was. For as for old ones that were before Wicliffe's days, they remain lawful, and be in some folk's hands'" (*Turning Points of English Church History*, pp. 200, 201).

Another Protestant writer, the late Dr. HOOK of Leeds, says: "It was not from hostility to a translated Bible, considered abstractedly, that the conduct of Wicliff, in translating it, was condemned. Long before his time there had been translators of Holy Writ. There is no reason to suppose that any objection would have been offered to the circulation of the Bible, if the object of the translator had only been the edification and sanctification of the reader. It was not till the designs of the Lollards were discovered, that Wicliff's version was proscribed" (*Lives of the Archbishops of Canterbury*, vol. iii. p. 83). Of the Lollards he says: "When we speak of them as martyrs, we ought to regard them as *political* martyrs rather than religious. They made religion their plea, in order to swell the number of the discontented; but their actions tended to a revolution in the State as well as in the Church... Both parties regarded their principles as subversive of all order, in things temporal as well as in things spiritual" (p. 94). (See also the Protestant Canon DIXON's *History of the Church of England from the Abolition of the Roman Jurisdiction*, vol. i. p. 451).

The same class of Protestant lecturers, above referred to, generally follow DAUBIGNÉ, the "Historian of the Reformation," in speaking of even the *Latin* Bible as "a rare book, unknown in those days" when Luther "discovered" a copy of the same in his monastery at Erfurt. This absurd falsehood was exposed, forty years ago, by Dr. MAITLAND, in the Appendix to his *Essays on the Dark Ages*; but even that learned writer gave but an imperfect list of the editions of the Latin Bible that had been published before the time of Luther's alleged "discovery"; whilst of the numerous Catholic *vernacular* versions of the Bible that had appeared before the year 1520 in Italy, Spain, France, Germany, and other countries of Europe, Dr. Maitland does not say a word.

REUSS, a leading Rationalist of Germany, says that "No book was so frequently published, immediately after the first invention of printing, as the Latin Bible; *more than one hundred editions* of it being struck off before the year 1520" (*Die Geschichte der Heiligen Schriften, N.T.* Brunswick, 1853, p. 458). HAIN, in his *Repertorium Bibliographicum*, printed at Tubingen, reckons consecutively *ninety-eight distinct editions before the year 1500*, independently of *twelve other editions*, which, together with the Latin text, presented the Glossa Ordinaria, or the Postillas of Lyranus. From the year 1475, when the first Venetian edition appeared, to the close of the century, that city alone yielded no fewer than *twenty-two complete editions* of the Latin Bible, besides some others with the notes of Lyranus.

I have elsewhere* given a list of the early Catholic *vernacular* versions of the Bible, part of which is appended to the present tract.

Writing in *The Academy* of August 7, 1886, Mr. KARL PEARSON says: "The Catholic Church has quite enough to answer for; ... but *in the fifteenth century it certainly did not hold back the Bible from the folk;* and it gave them in the vernacular a

---

* *Which is the True Church?* pp. 57—60.

long series of devotional works, which for language and religious sentiment have never been surpassed. Indeed, we are inclined to think it made a mistake in allowing the masses such ready access to the Bible. It ought to have recognized the Bible once for all as a work absolutely unintelligible without a long course of historical study; and, so far as it was supposed to be inspired, very dangerous in the hands of the ignorant."

Mr. Pearson seems here to have overlooked the fact—that no ill results had followed the authorized use of vernacular versions of the Bible amongst the Catholics of the fifteenth century. It was the religious *vertigo* consequent on the Protestant proclamation of "Liberty of Private Judgment," and the unbridled licentiousness which everywhere attended the footsteps of the "Reformers," that ought to have made it plain to all rational people on which side the misuse of the Bible really lay.

The evils which necessarily resulted from the first principle of Protestantism in regard to the Bible, were not slow in manifesting themselves. King HENRY VIII. himself declared in his last speech to Parliament: "I am extremely sorry to find how much the Word of God is abused, with how little reverence it is mentioned; how people squabble about the sense; how it is turned into wretched rhymes, sung and jangled in every alehouse and tavern: and all this in a false construction, and counter-meaning to the inspired writers. I am sorry to perceive the readers of the Bible discover so little of it in their practice: for I am sure charity was never in a more languishing condition, virtue never at a lower ebb, nor God Himself never less honoured and worse served in Christendom " (Collier's *Ecclesiast. Hist.* part ii. book iii. vol. v. p. 208, ed. Lond. 1852).

Before the end of the sixteenth century, 270 Protestant sects were enumerated by Staphylus and Cardinal Hosius. In our own country, at the present time, *Whitaker's Almanack* reckons about 200 Protestant denominations; but, according to a leading article in *The Times* of January 13, 1885, " England alone is reported to contain some *seven hundred* sects, each of whom proves a whole system of theology and morals from the Bible!" The Arian heresy, which, as HALLAM remarks, had been for centuries extinct, revived immediately after the appearance of Luther, and, under the name of Socinianism, has ever since been flourishing and spreading in all Protestant lands. In the present day, the two countries—Germany and England—which had always boasted most loudly of the "open Bible" of Protestantism, are foremost in manifesting the evidences of religious decay, and of wide-spread unbelief in the divine origin of the Christian Religion. Of *England* it was remarked by Canon MONEY, at the Plymouth Church Congress in 1876, that "However the sections of the working class might differ in intelligence, in sobriety, in honesty, they nearly all agreed in this—*they were alienated from Christianity. Barely 5 per cent. attended public worship.*" To which, in a paper read at the Leicester Church Congress (in 1880) he added: " It is well that we should think of Heathenism abroad, but we do not need to be constantly reminded of that Heathenism at home, which threatens to submerge this dear land of ours beneath a flood of ungodliness, vice, and intemperance." Of *Germany*, the *Edinburgh Review*, of October, 1880, remarked: " The land which was the cradle of the Reformation has become the grave of the Reformed faith. . . . All comparatively recent works on Germany, as well as all personal observation, tell the same tale. *Denial of every tenet of the Protestant faith among the thinking classes, and indifference in the masses, are the positive and negative agencies beneath which the Church of Luther and Melancthon has succumbed.* . . In contiguous parishes of Catholic and Protestant populations, one invariable distinction has long been patent to all eyes and conclusions. *The path to the Catholic Church is trodden bare, that to the Protestant Church is rank with grasses and weeds to the very door* " (pp. 530, 539).

We need say no more at present about " The Bible and the Reformation," or the misuse of the former by Protestants of all denominations. The few facts stated in this tract may at least suffice to recall to the minds of some earnest inquirers those solemn words of warning uttered by St. Peter—that "*No prophecy of Scripture is of any private interpretation*"* (2 St. Peter v. 20); and that in the Epistles of St. Paul "*are some things hard to be understood, which they that are unlearned and unstable wrest, as they do also the other Scriptures, unto their own destruction*" (2 St. Peter iii. 16).

But Protestants tell us that their Rule of Faith —" the Bible and the Bible only "—is expressly sanctioned in certain passages of the New Testament itself—viz., St. John v. 39; Acts xvii. 11; and 2 Tim. iii. 14. It is necessary, therefore, to say a few words on each of these texts.

I. The words "*Search the Scriptures*" (St. John v. 39), even if we admit this to be the correct translation of the Greek text, were not a command addressed to Christians, but simply a reproof to the *unbelieving Jews*, who,—glorying in their possession of, and strict adherence to, the sacred writings of the Old Testament, and erroneously and supersti-

---

* To escape the force of this text Protestants often allege that the words rendered "*private interpretation*" signify "*private divulgement*," *i.e.*, on the part of the prophet himself. But that standard Protestant work—*The Speaker's Commentary*—remarks: " The word rendered 'interpretation' is only found here in the New Testament, but the verb from which it is derived is used in St. Mark (iv. 34), ' He *expounded* all things to His disciples,' and that sense is no doubt the correct one " (Note *in loc.*). This is shown at greater length by the Protestant Bishop WORDSWORTH (*Greek Test.*, note *in loc.*), who also remarks that " this is the sense given to the word ἐπίλυσις in the *Vulgate, Syriac, Arabic, and Æthiopic Versions.*" He explains that St. Peter was warning his readers against a device of the Gnostic heretics, who " grounded their errors on arbitrary *false interpretations* of the word of prophecy; contravening the *public testimony* and received doctrine of the Universal Church of Christ."

tiously "*thinking* that *in them* they had eternal life,"—refused to receive that Divine Teacher Who was then present before them,—Who alone could give them eternal life,—and of Whom the Old Testament Scriptures plainly "gave testimony." "In *them*," said our Lord, "ye *think** that ye have eternal life; but ye will not come *unto Me* that ye may have life."

This text, however,—to which Protestants have during three centuries and a half so confidently appealed in support of their inadequate Rule of Faith,—is now generally acknowledged, by the best Protestant commentators themselves, to be a mistranslation. We are told by such high authorities as Bloomfield, Alford, *The Speaker's Commentary*, Bishop Ellicott's *Bible Commentary*, &c., that the passage should not be translated "*Search* the Scriptures" (in the imperative), but simply "*Ye search*" (*i.e.*, ye Jews *are in the habit of searching*) "the Scriptures, for in them ye think, &c." Thus rendered, the text implies the very opposite of what Protestants have generally sup-

---

* Throughout the Gospels, the Greek verb rendered "*to think*" is not once used affirmatively by Christ or the Evangelists as expressive of anything else than *an erroneous and unfounded opinion* —as in the following texts:—"They (the heathen) *think* that they shall be heard for their much speaking" (St. Matt. vi. 7); "*Think* not to say within yourselves, We have Abraham for our father" (St. Matt. iii. 3); "From him shall be taken even that which he *thinketh* he hath" (St. Luke viii. 18); "They *thought* that they had seen a Spirit" (St. Luke xxiv. 37); see also St. John xi. 13; xx. 15, &c. In all these passages the *same* Greek word is used as in Christ's reproof to the Jews:—"In the Scriptures ye *think* that ye have eternal life"; and in all of them *an erroneous and unfounded* opinion or thinking is denoted.

posed. "The intense, misplaced diligence of research," says the *Speaker's Commentary*, "is contrasted with the futile result." Dr. Ellicott remarks that "all the parallel verbs are in the Indicative"; and paraphrases the text:—"Ye search because ye think ye have: if ye were willing to come, ye should really have."

It may be added, that if the word "search" were imperative, it would be emphatic, and would signify:—"*Search* the Scriptures, your pretended highest, your exclusive authority,—to which you so confidently appeal to *disprove* My Divine mission (cf. St. John vii. 52): examine carefully your own witness; and you will find that this same witness,—this same Scripture,—*testifies of Me.*" "If ye had believed Moses, ye would have believed Me; for he wrote of Me" (v. 46).

II. Protestants appeal to Acts xvii. 11, where we read:—"*These* (the Jews of Beræa) *were more noble than those of Thessalonica, in that they received the word with all readiness of mind, and searched the Scriptures daily, whether those things were so.*" This is supposed to be a clear approbation of the Protestant principle that every individual should satisfy himself of the truth of any doctrine taught, by his own personal study and private interpretation of the Scriptures.

But this inference will not stand for a moment; for (1) the persons spoken of were not as yet Christians, but simply honest *Jewish inquirers* about the Christian religion; (2) the Scriptures referred to, consequently, were those of *the Old Testament alone;* (3) the *object* with which they searched these writings was that they might see whether St. Paul had rightly appealed to them in order to show that Jesus Christ was the true Messias (see verse 2). They did not "search the Scriptures" in order to learn all revealed truth (as Protestants pretend to do), but simply to satisfy themselves that He Whom Paul preached unto them was the Divinely commissioned Founder of that Church which the same Apostle elsewhere calls "the Pillar and Foundation of the truth."

The Protestant inference would prove far too much; for, as Cardinal Wiseman observes (*Lectures,* vol. i. p. 314), "These Beræans are supposed to be commended for searching in the Scriptures— to verify whose doctrines? Why, the very Apostles'! the very writers of the New Testament! Will any one push the principle of Bible-investigation to this point—to say that not even the word of an inspired Apostle was to be received, but was to be subjected to the private scrutiny of every ordinary Christian layman? Surely not: what then are we to understand by this passage? Clearly that persons *not yet* Christians, like the Jews of Beræa, and not convinced of the divine mission of those who preach to them, have a right, nay a duty of investigating the evidence which they bring. The Apostles, speaking to Jews, naturally appealed to the prophecies of the Old Testament, as the simplest and strongest evidence of the truth which they proclaimed. Their hearers naturally, and most justly verified their quotations, and satisfied themselves of their correct application. But surely when once convinced by these means, that those who addressed them were sent by God, this task was at an end; and nothing more remained, but that they should with docility attend to their teaching."

III. The third text cited by Protestants is 2 Tim. iii. 14, in which St. Paul says to Bishop Timothy:—"*From a child thou hast known the Holy Scriptures, which can instruct thee unto salvation by the faith that is in Christ Jesus. All Scripture, inspired by God, is profitable to teach, to reprove, to correct, to instruct in justice, that the man of God may be perfect, furnished unto every good work.*" On this text we remark—

1. That the Scriptures which Timothy had "known from a child" were the Jewish Scriptures of the Old Testament only; consequently St. Paul's words can have no reference to those of the *New* Testament,—regarding the preparation or circulation of which he does not give the slightest hint.

2. When he adds that these Scriptures of the Old Testament were "able to instruct Timothy unto salvation through the faith which is in Christ Jesus," he means simply that, by the study of the ancient prophecies, &c., Timothy had been led to find in our Lord the true Messias, and that, by embracing the faith which He revealed (and

which Timothy had learned, not from any written documents, but by the *oral* instruction of St. Paul himself,—whose "son in the faith" he was), he was truly "instructed or made wise unto salvation."

3. In the words which follow in the "Authorized Version,"—viz., "All Scripture *is* given by inspiration of God,"—there is a mistranslation,—corrected in the "Revised" Version. St. Paul does not say that "all Scripture (i.e., "*every writing*") is inspired,"—which would be nonsense; but that "all Scripture, inspired by God" (i.e., *which is* inspired by Him), is profitable, etc.

4. All Scripture, then, which is thus inspired "is profitable,"—but for whom, and for what purposes? St. Paul goes on to say:—"*to teach, to reprove, to correct, to instruct in justice, that the man of God may be perfect, furnished unto every good work.*" There is not a word in all this of the use of the Scriptures by the laity; and the purposes for which St. Paul here declares them to be "*profitable*" (observe, he does not say *all-sufficient*) are exclusively *the functions of the ministry*—"to teach, to reprove, to correct, etc.," and that the "*man of God*" (i.e. Timothy himself, or any other Christian Bishop or pastor; cf. 1 Tim. vi. 11) may become himself "perfect, furnished unto every good work."

No doubt the reading of the Holy Scriptures is also very *profitable* to intelligent and well-disposed laymen; but St. Paul does not say anything about it in this text; and what Protestants have to prove is—that such reading by the laity is not only *profitable*, but *necessary* and *all-sufficient* for their instruction in the whole revelation of Jesus Christ.

When citing these words, Protestants forget, also, that at that time nearly all of the New Testament Scriptures *had yet to be written;* and that after these writings did appear—one after another, at distant intervals of time, and addressed for the most part to particular individuals or congregations who had been already *orally* indoctrinated in the Christian religion—no provision whatever was made by the Apostles for their being *translated* into the languages of nations to whom Greek was an unknown tongue, or even for their *general diffusion* amongst the faithful of neighbouring Churches. It must be acknowledged that the private study of the Scriptures was altogether impossible in the case of those who did not possess them, or were unable to read them; and Protestants invariably keep out of sight the plain facts—that not only had the New Testament writings to be *collected, canonized* (i.e. separated from numerous spurious and heretical compositions that were attributed to the Apostles and their disciples, and inserted in the *Canon* of genuine Gospels and Epistles), *translated,* and *diffused* amongst all nations; but also that, previous to the invention of *printing*—which did not occur until the middle of the 15th century—not

The Bible and the Reformation. 19

one person in a thousand could possibly have *possessed* a copy of the Scriptures, or have READ it even had it been accessible to him.

But does not what has just been said tend to confirm the Protestant suspicion as to the Catholic Church's hostility to the reading of the Holy Scriptures by the laity in the present day? As a sufficient answer to this question I will merely cite the following passage from the *Pastoral Letter of all the Bishops of the United States, assembled in Plenary Council at Baltimore, in December*, 1884 :—

"But it can hardly be necessary for us to remind you, beloved brethren, that the most highly valued treasure of every family library, and the most frequently and lovingly made use of, should be the Holy Scriptures. Doubtless you have often read A'Kempis's burning thanksgiving to our Lord for having bestowed on us not only the adorable treasure of His Body in the Holy Eucharist, but also that of the Holy Scriptures, ' the Holy Books, for the comfort and direction of our life.' And you have before your eyes, prefixed to the Douay version of the Holy Bible, the exhortation of Pope Pius VI. in his letter to the Archbishop of Florence, that ' The faithful should be moved to the reading of the Holy Scriptures ; for these,' he says, 'are most abundant sources which ought to be left open to every one to draw from them purity of morals and of doctrine, to eradicate the

The Bible and the Reformation.

errors which are so widely disseminated in these corrupt times.' And St. Paul declares that 'What things soever were written, were written for our learning; that through patience and the comfort of the Scriptures we might have hope.' We hope that no family can be found amongst us without a correct version of the Holy Scripture."*

---

* In a Declaration of the principles of the Catholic Religion, published half a century ago by the ten Catholic Bishops, Vicars Apostolic in England and Scotland, it is said :

"As to translations of the Holy Scriptures into modern languages, the Catholic Church requires that none shall be put into the hands of the faithful but such as are acknowledged by ecclesiastical authority to be accurate, and conformable to the sense of the originals. There never was a general law of the Catholic Church prohibiting the reading of authorized translations of the Scriptures ; but considering that many, by their ignorance and evil dispositions, have perverted the meaning of the Sacred Text, to their own destruction, the Church has thought it prudent to make a regulation that the faithful should be guided in this matter by the advice of their respective Pastors." After further remarks, and after citing the Rescript of Pope Pius VII., dated April 18, 1820, and addressed to the Vicars Apostolic in England, the Bishops add : "But when the reading and the circulation of the Scriptures are urged and recommended as the entire Rule of Faith—as the sole means by which men are to be brought to the certain and specific knowledge of the doctrines, precepts, and institutions of Christ ; and when the Scriptures so read and circulated are left to the interpretation and private judgment of each individual ; then such reading, circulation, and interpretation are forbidden by the Catholic Church ; because the Catholic Church knows that the circulation of the Scriptures, and the interpretation of them by each one's private judgment, was not the means ordained by Christ for the communication of the true knowledge of His Law to all nations ; she knows that Christianity was established in many countries before one book of the New Testament was written ; that it was not by means of the Scriptures that the Apostles and their successors converted nations, or any one nation, to the unity of the Christian faith ; that the authorized reading and circulation of the Scriptures, and the interpretation of them by private judgment, are calculated to lead men to contradictory doctrines on the primary articles of Christian belief,—to inconsistent forms of worship, which cannot all be constituent parts of the uniform and sublime system of Christianity, to errors and fanaticism in religion, and to seditions and the greatest disorders in states and kingdoms."

EARLY CATHOLIC BIBLES IN THE VERNACULAR.

I. **German Bibles.**—The first German printed Bible, bearing the arms of Frederick III., issued from the Mentz press about 1462. Another version appeared in 1466, two copies of which are still preserved in the Senatorial Library at Leipsic. Other versions were published in rapid succession. "In the best biblical collection known," says Dr. E. S. Hall, "that of the King of Wurtemberg, at Stuttgart . . . there were when the learned librarian, Dr. Alder, published his great catalogue, *twenty-seven different editions of the Bible in German, printed before Luther's*, independently of the two in the library at Leipsic.* Many of these are not merely different editions, but different versions, as Cardinal Wiseman has remarked. In the 11th edition of Brockhaus's *German Cyclopædia*, published at Leipsic in 1868, in 15 vols., there are noticed 17 editions of the Bible in German, before the publication of Luther's. The last edition of *Chambers's Cyclopædia* gives the same number" ("*Who Translated the Bible?*" p. 156. Hobart Town, 1875).

* The CHURCH TIMES of July 26, 1878, speaking of the *List of Bibles in the Caxton Exhibition* (South Kensington, 1877), published by H. Stevens, says: "This catalogue will be very useful for one thing at any rate, as disproving the popular lie about Luther *finding* the Bible for the first time at Erfurt about 1507. Not only are there very many editions of the Latin Vulgate long anterior to that time, but there were actually nine GERMAN editions of the Bible in the Caxton Exhibition earlier than 1483, the year of Luther's birth, and at least three more before the end of the century." Mr. H. STEVENS writes in the ATHENÆUM of October 6, 1883, p. 434: "By 1507 more than one hundred Latin Bibles had been printed, some of them small and cheap pocket editions. There had been besides *thirteen editions of a translation of the Vulgate into German*, and others in other modern languages. . . . Among the most interesting editions latest made [to the Grenville Library in the British Museum] is a nearly complete set of fourteen grand old pre-Luther German Bibles, 1460—1518, all in huge folios except the twelfth, which is in quarto form."

The ATHENÆUM of December 22, 1883, contains an article on "The German Bible before Luther," in which it is shown that what Geffcken calls "the German Vulgate" was in common use among the people long before Luther's time; that Luther had evidently the old Catholic German Bible of 1483 before him, when making his translation; and that, consequently, "it is time we should hear no more of Luther as the first German Bible translator, and of his translation as an independent work from the original Greek."

II. Italian Bibles.—Three editions of the Bible printed in the Italian tongue appeared in the year 1471, one of which was from a translation made by Nicholas Malermi, a Camalodese monk, in 1421. No fewer than *eleven* complete editions of these versions appeared before the year 1500, and were reprinted *eight* times more before the year 1567, with the express permission of the Holy Office. At Venice, in 1486, there was also printed a translation of the Four Gospels; and in 1532 a new and complete Bible in Italian was published by Anthony Bruccioli, who professed to have translated direct from the original Hebrew and Greek. "In the space of twenty years," says Cardinal Wiseman, "it passed through *ten* editions, several of which—all very inaccurate—having been formally condemned, a revision was undertaken by Santes Marmoschini, a Dominican friar, but it grew under his hand into a new version, which was published at Venice in 1538, and again in 1546 and 1547." More than forty editions of the Bible in Italian are reckoned before the appearance of the first *Protestant* edition (which was little more than a reprint of Bruccioli's version), printed at Geneva in 1562 (See Le Long's *Bibliotheca Sacra;* Panzer's *Annales Typographici*, Nuremburg, 1791—1803; *Dublin Review*, vol. 1, etc.).

III. Spanish Bibles.—In Spain, the whole Bible, which had been translated into the vernacular tongue by Boniface Ferrier in 1405, was printed at Valencia in 1478, and reprinted in 1515, *with the formal consent of the Spanish Inquisition.* In 1512, the Gospels and Epistles were translated by Ambrosio de Montesina; and this work was reprinted at Antwerp, in 1544; at Barcelona, in 1601 and 1608; and at Madrid, in 1603 and 1615. Carranza, the celebrated Archbishop of Toledo, says in the Prologue to his Commentaries: "Before the heresies of Luther appeared, I do not know that the Holy Scriptures in the vulgar tongue were anywhere forbidden. In Spain, the Bible was translated into it by order of the Catholic sovereigns, at the time when the Moors and Jews were allowed to live among the Christians according to their own law." He then proceeds to show why the indiscriminate circulation of the same (from which so much evil resulted in other countries) was subsequently prohibited in Spain. (See Balmez on *European Civilization*, ch. 36, Eng. trans. p. 192).

IV. **French Bibles.**—A French translation of the New Testament, by two Augustinian friars, Julian Macho and Pierre Farget, was published at Lyons in 1478. A copy of this version is preserved in the Public Library at Leipsic. The French Bible of Guiars de Moulins was printed soon afterwards in a quarto edition; and, in 1487, a new edition, corrected and enlarged by Jean de Rely, afterwards Bishop of Angiers, was published at Paris under the auspices of Charles VIII. Before the year 1547 it passed through *sixteen* other editions—four at Lyons, and twelve at Paris. In 1512 Jacques Le Fevre undertook a new translation—the New Testament appearing at Paris in 1523; the Old, at Antwerp, in 1530, 1534, 1541. This version, corrected by the Louvain divines, became so popular that it passed through more than forty editions before the year 1700. Another French translation, by Nicholas de Leuse, was printed at Antwerp in 1534. The first *Protestant* version appeared at Neufchatel in 1535. (See Le Long's *Bibl. Sacr.; Dublin Review*, vol. i.; *Irish Ecclesiast. Record*, vol. i. &c.).

V. **Other Versions.**—Besides the German Bibles above mentioned, numerous DUTCH or FLEMISH versions were published towards the end of the 15th, or beginning of the 16th century. A new translation of the New Testament, by Cornelius Kendricks, was published in 1524, of which ten editions were published, at Antwerp alone, within thirty years. A BOHEMIAN version of the New Testament was published at Prague, in 1478 and 1488; at Cutra, in 1498; and at Venice, in 1506 and 1511. A POLISH version of the Bible was published at Cracow in 1556, 1577, 1599, 1619; another, by John Leopolita, appeared at Cracow in 1561. The translation by the Jesuit John Wujec, was issued between the year 1593 and 1599—accompanied with the Hebrew and Greek texts, &c. An ETHIOPIC Bible was published at Rome in 1548.

Although no Catholic version of the ENGLISH Bible appeared in print until some time after the publication of such versions in other countries, it is clear, from the testimony of Sir Thomas More above cited, that no *prohibition* of vernacular versions had been issued by the ecclesiastical authorities in this country, and that many *manuscript* copies of the same had been freely circulated, subsequently to, as well as "long before," the time of Wicliffe.

The Protestant Canon DIXON, of Carlisle, says: "From the earliest times the English Church or nation was possessed of the sacred writings through the labours of monks and bishops. . . . At length, however, at the beginning of the 15th century, the resolute prelate Arundel passed his famous Constitution to forbid any man from making new translations on his own account, or reading those that had been made in or since the time of the lately deceased Wicliffe. He thus proclaimed the war of authority against private versions; though certainly he neither forbade the ancient versions to be used, nor denied that an authorized version might be made. . . .

"It was TYNDALE and his fellow-labourers who awoke the question of translating the Scriptures, after the slumber of a century. The admirers and the guests of Germany, these voluntary exiles poured from their foreign refuges, upon their native land, an inexhaustible succession of printed versions of the various books of the Bible. These . . . were condemned by Convocation among the books of *mala dogmata*: they were seized or brought up by the Bishops, and committed to the flames. If the clergy had acted thus simply because they would have kept the people ignorant of the Word of God, they would have been without excuse. *But it was not so.* Every one of the little volumes containing portions of the Sacred Text, that was issued by Tyndale, contained also a prologue and notes written with such a hot fury of vituperation against the Prelates and clergy, the monks and friars, the rites and ceremonies of the Church, as . . . was hardly likely to commend it to the favour of those who were attacked. Moreover, the versions themselves were held to be hostile to the Catholic faith, as it was then understood, and to convey the sense unskilfully or maliciously" (*Hist. of the Church of England, from the Abolition of the Roman Jurisdiction*, vol. i. p. 451—2).

Was Barlow a Bishop?

BY MR. SERJEANT BELLASIS:

Being

Letters from an Anglican, since become a Catholic.

NOTE.

[The *Dictionary of National Biography* (vol. iv. p. 181), gives the following note as to the letters now here published for the first time in a separate form: "Mr. Serjeant Bellasis, while yet an Anglican, had, in 1847, written four letters on the question of Bishop Barlow's consecration, which, a few years afterwards, were published in a newspaper. A reprint of them, authorised by Bellasis, appeared in 1872 under the title 'Anglican Orders, by an Anglican, since become a Catholic,' 8vo, pp. 15." As a matter of fact there were only a few printer's sheets in existence during the Serjeant's lifetime, the reprint in question, for private circulation only, being undertaken some time after his death. The late Lord O'Hagan characterized the letters as being of "great historic interest," and they were known to the late Canon Estcourt, who alludes to their author in the preface to his work on Anglican Orders. Fr. Gallwey, S.J., had also access to them, but they were not very general, owing to the scarcity of the copies.—E. B.]

I.

LONDON, *April* 1, 1847.

My dear ——,
—The objections made by Roman Catholics to the validity of English Ordinations are threefold :—1st. That Archbishop Parker, from whom they are all derived, was never consecrated at all. 2nd. That the person who consecrated him (if he was consecrated) was not himself a consecrated Bishop. 3rd. That the form used was not such as to convey episcopal authority.

But they admit that if he was consecrated by a person who had himself been duly consecrated, and if a valid form was used, he was by such consecration a true Bishop, notwithstanding what they conceive to be the schism of the Anglican Church—that is, they believe that we Anglicans have preserved the Apostolical Succession in that case, although our Orders are irregular and schismatical.

The first charge is, that the records of the consecration of Archbishop Parker, which are at Lambeth Palace, are not genuine documents, but forgeries. These documents I saw yesterday, and my opinion is that they are genuine documents, although there certainly were grounds for suspicion, especially this—that when, at the time, the Catholics objected to Archbishop Parker that he had not been duly consecrated, he did not reply by producing the register of his consecration, which would have put the fact beyond dispute, but applied for and obtained an Act of Parliament to remedy any defects there might have been therein; and the register itself was not produced or specifically alluded to for more than fifty years after, and not until every one named in it was dead. However, notwithstanding this, I take it for granted that the register which I saw is true, and that Archbishop Parker underwent a form of consecration: it only remains, therefore, to make out that the person who consecrated him was himself a Bishop, and that he used a valid form.

On the accession of Queen Elizabeth there were fourteen Bishops in England. These, of course, were Catholic Bishops, and not one of them could be found who would consecrate the intended Archbishop. They were all deprived of their sees but one, and he refused to do it. This made it necessary to look about for some of the Bishops who had resigned or been deprived at the beginning of the reign of Mary, and the register at Lambeth states that Parker was consecrated by Bishop Barlow (who was Bishop of Bath and Wells at the accession of Mary, and who had resigned his see), assisted by Coverdale, Scory, and Hodgkins, three other deprived Bishops; and the question is, whether Barlow

Was Barlow a Bishop?

had ever himself been consecrated. I found, on reading both sides of the question, that what one stated as a fact the other denied, and so I determined to sift this question thoroughly, by reference to the actual documents, for myself; and I will now tell you honestly how the case stands.

I should tell you, *imprimis*, that at all consecrations one Bishop is called the consecrating Bishop, and the others are called the assistants. Now, the register at Lambeth states that Barlow was the consecrating Bishop, assisted by the others; and this it is which makes Barlow's own consecration so important, because all our present Bishops have been consecrated by persons who primarily trace back their succession through Parker, and consequently through Barlow.

Bishop Barlow's history is this, that he was consecrated Bishop of St. Asaph in 1536; that subsequently to his consecration he was translated in the same year to St. David's; that in 1548 he was again translated to Bath and Wells, which he resigned on the accession of Queen Mary; that he went abroad, and returned on the accession of Elizabeth, and then consecrated Parker. The question is, was he (Barlow) ever *consecrated?* as it is not doubted that he did occupy all the above sees in succession.

First, it appears from Rymer that he was *elected* Bishop of St. Asaph in January 1535-6, and the mandate for his consecration is dated February 2nd, 1536; but although Cranmer's Register at Lambeth is very minute and perfect in recording all the consecrations of Bishops in his province during his Archiepiscopate, there is no record of the consecration of Barlow, which of itself throws a doubt upon it. All the other documents are there—his election, confirmation, &c., &c.; but where in other cases the account of the consecration follows, in his case it is omitted.

But this might have been an accidental omission: let us see, then, what the circumstances were as to his being made Bishop of St. Asaph.

The mandate to Cranmer to consecrate him Bishop

of *St. Asaph* is dated Feb. 2nd, 1536; on the 18th Feb. the Bishop of *St. David's* died, and to his Bishopric of St. David's Barlow was transferred, and the question is, *Was he consecrated before he was transferred?* I have seen the *congé d'élire* or licence to the Dean and Chapter of St. Asaph to elect another Bishop in the room of Barlow. Now, these licences to elect always specify the cause of the vacancy; it is always, if the previous Bishop is dead, "vacante per mortem naturalem ultimi Episcopi;" if he is translated to another see, it is "per *translationem* ultimi Episcopi;" if he has been deprived "per deprivationem ultimi Episcopi." Also a Bishop who has been elected and not consecrated is always, in all formal documents, called "Bishop elect" only. Now, in the *congé d'élire* to the Dean and Chapter of St. Asaph to elect a Bishop in the room of Barlow, he (Barlow) is called "Bishop elect," and the cause of the vacany is said to be his *exchange*. The words are "vacante per liberam *transmutationem* Wilhelmi Barlow ultimi Episcopi *electi*," and he is so described throughout the whole of the formal documents relating to the election of his successor. There is no other instance in which a *translation* is described by any other word than "translationem," nor in which a *consecrated* Bishop to any see is called a "Bishop *elect.*" The conclusion is, therefore, I think, not an improbable one, that in consequence of the Bishopric of St. David's falling vacant when Barlow was about to be consecrated to St. Asaph, the consecration did not take place; but the "Bishop elect" of St. Asaph—viz., Barlow—was "exchanged to St. David's."

It is also important to remark that the documents contained in the same register of Cranmer relating to the election of Barlow's successor at St. Asaph's (Robert Wharton) conclude with the usual register of *his* consecration.

Another reason why it is likely that Barlow was not consecrated for St. Asaph is, that it appears by Strype's *Memorials*, vol. i., pt. 1, p. 347, that Thomas Holcroft and Wm. Barlow, Bishop *elect* of St. Asaph, were sent by Henry VIII. into Scotland on a mission to King James, to induce him to throw off the Pope's authority. Now, if he went to Scotland as Bishop elect, he could scarcely have returned in time to have been consecrated *under the mandate of February 2nd.*

I have no time to write more to-day. The above are the reasons why it is, as I think, almost if not quite certain that Barlow was not consecrated Bishop of St. Asaph: it remains to be seen whether it is likely that he was afterwards consecrated either at St. David's or at Bath and Wells.

Yours most sincerely,
EDWARD BELLASIS.

II.

April 8, 1847.

Dear ——,

—I have been so busy all the week, that I have not been able to continue my letter to you till now, I told you in my last letter that it was very probable, if not certain, that Barlow never was consecrated Bishop of *St. Asaph.*

1st. Because there is no register of his consecration at Lambeth, although all other formal documents are there relating to the election;

2nd. Because in the document relating to his successor, Barlow is invariably stated to have been "Bishop elect" only;

3rd. Because the occasion of vacancy in those documents is not expressed in the usual word, "translation," but by other words which are not to be found in any other case before or since, and which imply exchange, or something short of any ordinary "translation," which is the term applied to the removal of an actual Bishop from one see to another.

I subjoin the ordinary form—the invariable form, in fact—in which, when the cause of the vacancy is the removal of the late Bishop to another see, that cause is expressed in the formal documents.

"Vacante per translationem Domini A. B., ultimi Episcop. ibidem."

In the election documents of Barlow's successor at St. Asaph, the cause of vacancy is expressed several times over; and I subjoin the different modes in which it is expressed in the different documents.

Letters patent.—(Cran. Reg. 194-a.)

"Per liberam transmutacionem Willi'mi Barlowe, ultimi Ep'i ib'm el'ci.

Petition.—(Cran. Reg. 194-b.)

"Per cessionem, dimissionem, sive transmutacionem Reverendi Patris D'ni Will'mi Barlowe, ultimi Epis. elect ib'm."

Instrument of assent.—(C. R. 195-b.)

"Per liberam dimissionem, cessionem, et transmutacionem Reverendi Patris D'ni Will'mi Barlowe, ultimi Episcopi ib'm electi."

Process of Election.—(C. R. 195-b.)

"Per liberam renunciationem, cessionem, sive transmutacionem Reverendi Patris D'ni Will'mi Barlowe, ultimi et immediati Ep'i ib'm in eadem Eccl'ia Cath. Assaphen electi."

In the same.—(C.R. 196-a.)

"Per transmutationem, cessionem, sive liberam dimissionem Reverendi Patris D'ni Will'mi Barlowe, ultimi Præsulis sive Pastoris electi."

In the same.—(Cran. Reg. 196-b.)

"Per liberam renunciationem, cessionem, dimissionem, et transmutationem D'ni Will'mi Barlowe, ultimi et immediati P'sulis et Pastoris et Ep'i ejusdem electi."

Final sentence.—(C.R. 197-b.)

"Per liberam transmutacionem Dn'i Will'mi Barlowe, ultim. Ep'i ib'm electi et confirmati."

Suppose, then, that Barlow was not consecrated at St.

Asaph, that is, as Bishop of that see—was he consecrated on his " transmutation " to St. David's ?

Cranmer's register contains, p. 205-b and in the following pages, the formal documents of the removal of Barlow to St. David's. All is perfect, but there is no record of consecration. This, however, is accounted for by the fact that throughout all these documents he is described " nuper Episcopus Assaphen : " that is he is no longer called " Bishop elect," but is assumed to be a complete Bishop, and as such is elected and confirmed in his new see, without any record of any consecration.

I am now going down to Lambeth to see if there is any trace of his consecration when he was removed to Bath and Wells.

Believe me, yours most sincerely.

EDWARD BELLASIS.

III.

April 13, 1847.

Dear——,

—I went on Saturday again to Lambeth to search the Register respecting Bishop Barlow. There is, however, no trace of any consecration on his removal to the see of Bath and Wells in 1548 ; therefore, so far as the register is concerned, he does not appear to have been consecrated at all.

But it may be said, that as it appears that Barlow himself was one of the assistant Bishops at the consecration of Bulkeley, Bishop of Bangor, in 1541 [Cran. Reg. 272], it is very improbable that he should have allowed so important a ceremony to have remained unperformed in his own case, and also it is improbable that Cranmer, whose duty it was to consecrate him, should have neglected to do so. This would be a very important argument as to probabilities, if it should appear that Cranmer, who ought to have consecrated, and Barlow, who ought to have been consecrated, were at the time convinced of the necessity of consecration to the valid making of a Bishop; but supposing it to be proved that both of them had at that time deliberately expressed their opinion that consecration was unnecessary, it would confirm the probability that in Barlow's case it had not been done.

In the reign of Henry VIII. certain questions were put by the King to the then Bishops and other divines upon certain theological points; and these questions, and the answers of the different Bishops and others, are to be found in Burnet's *History of the Reformation*, vol. i., p. 201. Amongst others are the following :—

Question—" Whether the Apostles lacking a higher power, as in not having a Christian King among them, made Bishops by that necessity, or by authority given of God."

CRANMER—"The civil ministers under the King be Lord Chancellor, Lord Treasurer, Admirals, Sheriffs, &c., the ministers of God's Word under his Majesty be Bishops, Parsons, Vicars, and such other Priests as be appointed by his Highness to that ministration—as, for example, the Bishop of Canterbury, the Bishop of Durham, the Parson of Winwick, &c. All the said offices be appointed, assigned, and elected in every place by the laws and orders of Kings and Princes. In the admission of many of these officers be divers comely ceremonies and solemnities, and which be not of necessity, but only for a good order and seemly fashion; for if such officers and ministrations were committed without such solemnity, they were nevertheless duly committed, and there is no more promise of God that grace is given in the committing of the ecclesiastical office than it is in the committing of the civil office."

BARLOW—" Because they lacked a Christian Prince, by that necessity they ordained other Bishops."

Question—"Whether Bishops or Priests were first; and if the Priest was first, then the Priest made the Bishop?"

CRANMER—"The Bishops and Priests were at one time, and were no two things, but both one office, at the beginning of Christ's religion."

BARLOW—"At the beginning they were all one."

Question—"Whether in the New Testament *be required any consecration* of a Bishop or Priest, or only appointing to the office be sufficient?"

CRANMER—"In the New Testament he that is appointed to be a Bishop or a Priest *needeth no consecration* by the Scripture, for *election or appointment thereto is sufficient*."

BARLOW—"Only the appointing."

Beside these opinions so expressed, articles were exhibited against Barlow in November, 1536 (that is, in the same year in which he was removed to St. David's), by the Catholics, for having said as follows in a sermon :—

"If the King's Grace, being supreme head of the Church of England, did choose, denominate, and elect any layman being learned to be a Bishop, that he so chosen (without mention made of any orders) should be as good a Bishop as he is, or the best in England."

So much for the opinions of Barlow as to the necessity of consecration.

But it may be said again, notwithstanding their private opinions, it is not likely that any Bishop would remain unconsecrated, although he might think it not necessary. There is, however, an instance in Cranmer's register of a Bishop being elected and confirmed, and remaining Bishop of a see for a year unconsecrated, and then being consecrated upon his translation to a more prominent see. Bonner was elected and confirmed Bishop of Hereford in October, 1538 [Cran. Reg. 218], but there is no register of his consecration at that time; but in October, 1539, he is translated to London and in April, 1540, and not before, he is consecrated as Bishop of London [Cran. Reg. 241], having remained, therefore, Bishop of Hereford a year and Bishop of London half a year without being consecrated.

Under all these circumstances, considering the openly expressed opinions of both Cranmer and Barlow that consecration was not necessary—that that opinion would be pleasing to King Henry—that there is no record of any consecration of Barlow by Cranmer or any one commissioned by him, or by any one at all—that the documents relating to the election of his successor at St. Asaph speak of Barlow as having been "Bishop-elect" only, and use words to describe the cause of the vacancy altogether unusual and implying something short of a regular "translation,"—I think it is in the highest degree probable, if not certain, that Barlow never was consecrated at all; and if so, it follows that he had no power to consecrate others, and therefore that Parker's consecration, so far as it depends upon Barlow, was no consecration at all.

In addition to these considerations, it may be important to know whether there existed any misgiving at the time of the consecration of Archbishop Parker as to the power of Barlow and the other Protestant Bishops to consecrate. It appears that Cardinal Pole, the last Archbishop, being dead, Queen Elizabeth issued a Commission to William Barlow and John Scory to consecrate Parker, joining with them in the same commission four of the Catholic Bishops. These four did not act, probably would not; but whatever their reasons might have been, a second Commission was issued six weeks later to Barlow, Scory, and some other Protestant Bishops including with them one of the above four Catholic Bishops, viz., the Bishop of Landaff (he eventually refused to act), and that second Commission contained the following clause, which was never heard of in any such Commission before or since :—

"Supplentes nihilominus, suprema auctoritate nostrâ Regiâ—si quid, aut in hiis, quæ juxta mandatum, nostrum prædictum, per vos fient, aut *in vobis aut vestrum aliquo conditione, statu, facultate vestris* ad premissa perficienda, *desit aut deerit* eorum, quæ, per statuta hujus regni, *aut per leges Ecclesiasticas* in eâ parte requiruntur aut necessaria sunt, temporis ratione et rerum necessitate id postulante."

This seems to imply that it was supposed at the time that there were defects or deficiencies of some kind requiring such a clause.

This, therefore, is the state of the case so far as Barlow is concerned; and *if it be true that the consecrating Bishop* must be a true Bishop *in order to make the consecration valid*, and that it is not sufficient that the assistant Bishops alone should be true Bishops, then the existence of the Apostolical succession amongst ourselves depends upon the fact whether Barlow (who was, as appears by the register, the consecrating Bishop of Parker) had or not been consecrated.

Suppose, however, that this is not so, and that it is quite sufficient if any one of the assistant Bishops at a consecration be a true Bishop, and suppose that there was one true Bishop among the assistants at Parker's consecration, then the question arises whether the form used was a valid form, and that point I must leave for the present.

Believe me, yours most sincerely,
EDWARD BELLASIS.

IV.

Easter Eve, 1847.

My dear——,
—I perceive in my last letter that I assume, without proving, that Barlow was the consecrating

Bishop at Parker's consecration; I therefore subjoin, first, the rubric in the old Catholic service which makes the distinction between the consecrating Bishop and the assistants; and, secondly, the account given in Parker's register at Lambeth of the part taken by Barlow, as distinguished from the others, on the occasion of Parker's consecration.

CATHOLIC RUBRIC.

"The officiating Bishop then goes to the altar, where being seated in a chair, with his face turned towards the people, the assistant Bishops lead to him him that is to be consecrated, conducting him between them, and the elder of the assistant Bishops, addresses himself to the consecrating Bishop and says to him in Latin, 'Reverendissime Pater, postulat sancta Mater Ecclesia Catholica ut hunc præsentem Presbyterum ad onus episcopatûs sublevetis.'"

The register of Lambeth then describes this part of Parker's consecration :—

"Finito tandem Evangelio, Hereford'en electus, Bedford'en suffraganeus, et Milo Coverdale (de quibus supra) Archiep'um coram Cicestren electo [Barlow] apud mensam in cathedra sedente, hiis verbis adduxerunt Reverende in Deo Pater, hunc virum p'm [pium] pariter atq: doctum *tibi* offerimus atq; p'ntamus [presentamus] ut Archiep'us consecretur."

It is obvious, therefore, that the same distinction was made at Parker's consecration that was accustomed; viz., that one of the Bishops present (in this case, Barlow, Bishop-elect of Chichester,) was the chief officiating Bishop, the other assisting Bishops bringing and offering the new Bishop to him for consecration.

Both in the Catholic service and in the Anglican, notwithstanding that one of the Bishops is considered and called the consecrating Bishop, all the Bishops present lay their hands upon the Bishop to be consecrated, and repeat the words appointed to be said,* and some say that if any one of the persons who so lays his hands on the new Bishop is a properly-consecrated

* This is not quite accurate. The Anglican rubric orders that the consecrator *alone* should repeat the words of consecration.— J. D. B.

Bishop, the consecration is valid: this point I do not pretend to discuss, nor am I qualified to do so.

The case, therefore, at present stands thus: if it is necessary that the principal consecrating Bishop should have been himself consecrated, and if Barlow never was consecrated, then our whole hierarchy falls to the ground; but supposing it is sufficient that any one of the Bishops present and assisting should be a true Bishop, and that it does not depend upon the consecrating Bishop alone, then the only question is, was a valid form used in Parker's case?

This point I must postpone till I understand the question better than I do at present.

Yours most sincerely,
EDWARD BELLASIS.

V.

May 3, 1847.

My dear――,
 ―There are a few other facts and considerations in relation to what I have already written which I will give you at once whilst they are in my memory, although they may be somewhat unconnected.

As to the validity of the consecration depending upon the consecrating Bishop. Cranmer, at one period of his Episcopate, as you will see by my index to his register of consecrations, rarely consecrated in his own person; he issued a commission in each case to some one to consecrate in his place. This commission, however, is ordinarily only addressed to one Bishop. No one has a right to consecrate in a province but an archbishop: if the assistant Bishops, therefore, are also consecrators, it may be said they should be included by name in the Commission.

Again, the consecrating Bishop is the party who examines the Bishop elect, and so may be said to take the responsibility of the consecration. But this is a matter that must really be left to divines to determine. I perceive, however, that it is said on the Anglican side, "Why do the assistant Bishops lay their hands on the head of the Bishop to be consecrated, if they do not by that act consecrate?" To which it is replied on the other, "They do so as witnesses and to signify their assent, in the same way as the Priests present lay their hands on with the Bishop at ordinations of Priests."

You must take all I say as a mere statement of facts: it is possible that other documents may exist which may show Barlow to have been consecrated; all I say is, that after a diligent search I have discovered nothing at present but what leads to the conviction that he never was.

Yours most sincerely,
EDWARD BELLASIS.

To the argument contained in the foregoing letters it has been observed:—

1. That the suggestion of Barlow not being consecrated was not made until 48 years after his death.

Answer—It was only when the state of the public records became known that the doubt arose.

2. Consecration must be presumed until disproved.

Answer—True: *primâ facie* case of non-consecration must be made out: but this being done, the *onus probandi* lies on the other side.

3. Neither Cranmer nor Barlow durst have run such a risk with a monarch like Henry VIII.

Answer—Non-consecration would be personally agreeable to the King, who held that consecration was not necessary, and whose power was increased by its omission. If there was no consecration, the fact was probably known to him, and the rite omitted in order to please him.

4. The non-consecration would have been known and mentioned in controversy against Barlow in his lifetime, which it never was.

Answer—The same reasons which prevailed for making the fact known to the King would obtain for concealing it from the public, amongst whom, no doubt, a strong Catholic feeling still prevailed, which would not have endured an unconsecrated Bishop.

The grounds for at least doubting Barlow's consecration are:—

1. That it is plain from the public records relating to his successor at St. Asaph, that he was not consecrated as Bishop of that See.

2. That it is plain from all the documents relating to his election and confirmation at St. David's that he was treated as if he had been a consecrated Bishop before his election to that See.

So *primâ facie* he was not consecrated at all; a conclusion confirmed by his and Cranmer's declared opinions as to the non-necessity of consecration.

EDWARD BELLASIS.

ADDENDUM.

(Extract from a Letter.)

VILLA STE. CÉCILE, HYÈRES, VAR.
March 26th, 1872.

It is not a question of the mere omission of a record of Barlow's consecration; but if the records as they exist are true, he could not have been consecrated at all.

1. It is quite plain that his successor was appointed to St. Asaph as succeeding an unconsecrated Bishop; therefore, Barlow was not consecrated as Bishop of St. Asaph.

2. On his removal to St. David's he was not consecrated; all the formal documents are perfect, and there is no record of consecration, indeed he is throughout spoken of as the "late Bishop of St. Asaph."

3. Barlow, in going through the form of consecrating Archbishop Parker, could not have had the "intention" necessary for a valid act, as he did not believe there was any difference between a Priest and a Bishop, and the form had been altered so as to avoid admitting it.

EDWARD BELLASIS.

WAS BARLOW EVER CONSECRATED AS BISHOP OF ST. DAVID'S?

Sergeant Bellasis has clearly proved from Cranmer's register that up to the day of his election as Bishop of St. David's, Barlow was only Bishop *elect* of St. Asaph's. He was elected to St. David's April 10th, 1536. His election was confirmed April 21st. He received the grant of the temporalities of St. David's, April 26th, and from that time styled himself, and was styled, "Bishop" of St. David's. He was summoned to Parliament as "Bishop" of St. David's, April 27th. He was enthroned May 1st, and took his seat in the House of Lords, June 30th. It is not pretended by any one that he was consecrated after taking his seat in the House of Lords. Was he consecrated before the 30th of June?

Dr. Lee claims that he must have been consecrated on Sunday, April 23rd, because he received the grant of his temporalities on April 26th;* but this is purely a gratuitous conjecture which has no evidence to support it whatever. We know from Cranmer's register that only four consecrations of Bishops are recorded to have taken place in the year 1536, none of them on April 23rd.† Moreover the very grant of restitution of temporalities relied on to prove his consecration clearly proves the contrary. It is not in the usual form by any means. From the year 1534, the date of the abolition

---

* *Validity of the Holy Orders of the Church of England*, p. 167. London, 1869.

† The episcopal consecrations for the year 1536 were held on March 19th, June 11th, July 2nd, and Oct. 22nd. Stubbs' *Registrum Sacrum*, pp. 77-78.

of the Papal Supremacy down to the abolition of *congé d'élire* under Edward VI., it was usual to recite in the grant of temporalities that all the conditions necessary to a legal and valid consecration—viz., *congé d'élire*, election, royal assent, confirmation, investiture, with the episcopal insignia and the accepted homage and fealty of the nominee—had been complied with. The fact of consecration was always insisted on. For instance, Rymer (xiv. p. 552) gives the mandate for the consecration of Edward Fox to the See of Hereford as follows:—" By this writ we command that you confirm the election and the person of the elect with all convenient despatch, and that you duly import to the same, and to his person, the *gift of consecration*, as it is meet; and that you do, and execute all other and singular things pertaining to, or which may in any way pertain, together, or successively, to the conferring of such confirmation and *consecration*." Then follows the grant of the temporalities of the See:—"Whereas the most Rev. Father in Christ, Thomas, Archbishop of Canterbury, hath *consecrated* Edward Fox a Bishop, and hath invested him with episcopal insignia, as it appeareth from his letters patent directed unto us. We, &c."

Compare these with the mandate and grant of restitution in Barlow's case. Cranmer (Register p. 281, also Rymer xiv. p. 559) gives the words of Barlow's mandate thus:—"And this we signify unto you by the tenor of these presents, that in this matter you do what belongs to your office." Such are the orders of the King to Cranmer; nothing more, not a word about consecration. The wording of the grant of temporalities of St. David's given by Estcourt (p. xix) is equally remarkable. It is not the usual grant made to a Bishop after his consecration, but a "grant of the custody of the temporalities on account of the *vacancy* of the See" to Barlow and his assigns " during his life," thus rendering a grant of temporalities after consecration unnecessary. Such grants were sometimes made to a Bishop-elect before consecration, but never to a consecrated Bishop. This grant recites the fact of Barlow's nomination, election, and confirmation, but there is not a word about consecration. It says:—" Henry VIII. &c. To all, &c. Know ye, that whereas the Cathedral Church of St. David's has, by the death of Richard Rawlins, late Bishop of St. David's, been widowed and deprived of pastoral comfort, and is thereby vacant; and whereas on that account all the proceeds and profits, farm rents, reversions together with the beneficial uses and temporal emoluments of the said bishopric have belonged and accrued to us, by the right of our royal prerogative and the same are known to belong and accrue; and whereas the Precentor and Chapter of the said cathedral church, after the death of the aforesaid Bishop, with our previous license, have chosen for their Bishop and pastor, our well beloved and faithful William Barlow, *named by us Bishop*, and whereas the most Reverend Father in Christ, Thomas, Archbishop of Canterbury, hath *accepted* and *confirmed* that election; and hath *set over* the aforesaid church of St. David's, the said Bishop so elected as appeareth by the letters patent of the said Archbishop to us directed, we now for certain causes and considerations *specially* moving us and for the sincere affection, which we have and bear towards the *aforesaid Bishop*, have, hereby, with special favour and with certain knowledge and of our own free act, given and granted, and do by these presents give and grant in our own part, and for our heirs and successors to the same *now Bishop*, all and singular the issues and lands, &c., during his life. In testimony whereof, &c., April 26th."*

This document not only clearly proves that Barlow was not consecrated up to April 26th, but also supplies the motive for his not being consecrated subsequently. The royal theologian has left it in writing, that in virtue of his supremacy over the Church of England he claimed the right to make Bishops by royal nomination without consecration. Cranmer fully endorsed this view, and

* See Memoranda Roll of the Lord High Treasurer's Remembrancer 28. Henry VIII., Easter turn Roll. I.

had probably suggested it to his royal master. He lays down (Burnet's *History of the Reformation*, i. p. 201) that "the ministry of God's word under his Majesty be Bishops, Parsons, and such other Priests as be *appointed* by his Highness, to that ministration—as, for example, the Bishop of Canterbury, the Bishop of Durham, the Parson of Winwick, &c., all the said offices be appointed, assigned, and elected, in every place by the laws and orders of Kings and Princes. In the admission of many of these offices, be divers comely ceremonies and solemnities, and *which be not of necessity*, but only for a good order and seemly fashion, for if such offices and ministrations were committed *without* such solemnities they were nevertheless *duly* committed, and there is no more promise of God that grace is given in the committing of the ecclesiastical office than it is in the committing of the civil office." In this grant of temporalities this royal claim to make a Bishop by nomination is set forth in all its naked Erastianism. The King says that he has named Barlow Bishop, that Cranmer has confirmed him, and that, therefore, he is now Bishop. For anyone after this to have questioned the validity of Barlow's episcopal character would have exposed him to the penalties for denying the Royal Supremacy, and no one who did not ambition the fate of a Fisher or a More, would care to expose himself to the consequences of doing so. This document therefore supplies the answer to the question so often asked—what motive could Barlow have had for wishing to shirk consecration?

In the face of these and other facts, Haddon is obliged to admit that the fact that Barlow was not consecrated before June is "almost certain."*

Haddon argues that Barlow must have been consecrated on June 11th, along with Repps of Norwich, because that is the only day in June on which any consecration is recorded to have taken place; so that if he was not consecrated then, he was not consecrated

---

* Bramhall's Works, iii. preface: *Anglo-Catholic Library.*

in June at all: and there is no mention of Barlow having been present in the record of the consecration held on June 11th.

But this is drawing a conclusion without proving your major premiss, in fact from a mere assumption. Repps took his seat with Barlow in the House of Lords June 30th: had they been consecrated together Barlow would have taken precedence, because he was elected April 10th, confirmed April 21st, summoned to the House April 27th, and enthroned May 1st, whereas Repps was not elected Bishop till May 31st. The precedence was, however, given to Repps, which proves that they had not been consecrated together, and that Barlow took his seat as "custos spiritualitatis" rather than as a consecrated Bishop. Haddon's surmise has been pulverized by the discovery of Cromwell's warrant in the office of the Exchequer to the Garter King at Arms* for the payment of Barlow's "dyetts" and in this warrant, which is dated June 12th, Barlow is described as still "elect of St. David's." Now Cromwell not only was intimate with Barlow, but was the King's Vicar General, and therefore his evidence is conclusive that Barlow had not been consecrated on June 11th. This document gives the *coup de grace* to the Anglican contention, for it is not claimed that any episcopal consecration was held between June 12th and June 30th, nor is it contended that Barlow was consecrated after he took his seat in the House of Lords.

Besides, we have the very striking evidence of Barlow's register taken in connection with what has been already stated. Mr. Bailey in his *Defence of Holy Orders in the Church of England*, (p. 45.) says:—"We admit that in Cranmer's register the consecration of Barlow is not to be found, but his confirmation only (although the half page following the confirmation being left vacant affords a reasonable supposition that it was omitted by the fault of the registrar whose duty it was to enter it); but neither are those of many other Bishops

* Ashmolean MS. no. 157, fol. 48, Bodleian, Oxon.

whose consecration has never yet been doubted by anyone." The writer here, like Haddon, takes for granted the fact in dispute, which has to be proved. The supposition that the entry was omitted by the fault of the registrar is not at all reasonable. All the other entries about Barlow are made with the greatest care and exactness and the fact that the registrar left a space vacant to enter his consecration when it took place proves that Barlow had not been consecrated when the other entries were made. And the evidence already adduced goes to show that no entry was made, simply because there was nothing to enter. Barlow's case is entirely different from that of Bishops whose registers are lost. In such cases we could not infer anything from that fact, if their views were orthodox about consecration. Barlow's register is not lost, and is positive evidence against him. Had he been consecrated, the presumption is the fact would have been recorded in the same way that the other facts about his appointment have been recorded. The fact that it is not recorded is under the circumstances a piece of strong corroborative evidence that it never took place at all. Haddon points out that the consecrations of Fox of Hereford, Latimer of Worcester, Sampson of Chichester, Helsey of Rochester, Skyp of Hereford, and Bell of Worcester, are not entered in Cranmer's register. No one has ever questioned the fact that they were consecrated. Why then should the fact of Barlow's consecration be questioned? Because there is no parity between the cases. The consecrations of these six Bishops can be proved from other sources. Fox's consecration is entered in his register thus: "Consecrated 26 Sept., 1535, by the Archbishop of Canterbury and the Bishops of Winchester and Salisbury in the Cathedral of Winchester." (Fox's register at the end of Booth's Richardson's.) Latimer's consecration is attested by letters patent from Cranmer in his restitution of temporalities given by Rymer (xiv. 553). Sampson's consecration is attested in the same way; see Rymer xiv. 573. Helsey's consecration is attested in the same way; see

Rymer xiv. 553 and also by his own register given by
Richardson (537) date 18 Sept. 1535., Skyp's consecration is attested by a royal licence given by Rymer
(xiv. 648), and also by the Hereford register. Bell's
consecration is also attested in his restitution of temporalities given by Rymer (xiv. 642) by letters patent
from Cranmer. On the other hand no evidence from
any source whatever can be produced to show when,
where, or by whom Barlow was consecrated. The only
date suggested with any show of reason when he could
possibly have been consecrated, 11th June, is proved by
Cromwell's warrant to be out of the question. It is
this that gives such significance to the blank space in
his register, which has remained a blank space to the
present day.

In Mary's reign, Barlow promptly resigned and betook
himself to the Continent, thereby avoiding all question being raised as to his episcopal character. In
Elizabeth's time the question of his episcopal status
comes up again. We have an official document in
the Record Office* dated Oct., 1559, in which Queen
Elizabeth distinctly states that Barlow still remained
"unconsecrated." This in connection with a man
with such a history as Barlow's is not without significance. Of course it may be that, owing to the loose
notions about consecration then current, too much
stress cannot be laid upon the use of such terms. But

---

* State Papers Dom. Eliz. vii. p. 19. also Parker's Correspondence p. 101. It is sometimes objected that this statement proves
nothing, because Scory is classed among the unconsecrated as well
as Barlow, and he was certainly consecrated by the Anglican rite.
But this argument seems to tell the other way. The Royal Commission appointed by Queen Mary to deal with such Anglican
Prelates, deposed them on account of *nullity* of consecration; and
Queen Mary's first Parliament had decreed that everything done
about Anglican ordinations in the previous reign was null and void
and of no effect. Scory, therefore, was, in the eyes of the law,
which was still unrepealed, no more a consecrated Bishop than
Hooper and Finer who had been degraded only from the priesthood
before execution. However, both Barlow and Scory are classed
with others who were certainly unconsecrated.

there is the fact and it may be, that although Barlow was recognised as being still unconsecrated in 1559, on the principle of *quieta non movere*, it was thought best for public reasons, to let the matter drop, especially as Parker and his followers had no faith in the necessity of episcopal consecration.

The evidence of the Lambeth Register is however not easy to get over. That curious document proves that the compilers were fully aware that the question of Barlow's episcopal character was an awkward one, which they did not quite know how to deal with. Canon Estcourt has proved that the present copy of the Lambeth Register is not the original record but a compilation from it in which certain important facts are carefully glossed over or suppressed. In the British Museum is preserved amongst the Harleian MSS. (419 p. 149,) a document called Foxe's MSS. which appears to be a copy of the original entry. If this is compared with the present official compilation, some very important alterations are apparent. In the former we are told that Barlow was Parker's consecrator and the other prelates were his assistants, quite in accordance with traditional usage. In the official copy this is altered, and Parker is represented as having had four consecrators instead of one consecrator and three assistants. There must have been some reason for this alteration. What was it? Why is the rubric in the Anglican ordinal, which was ordered to be followed on that occasion and which the Lambeth Register states was followed, represented as having been disregarded? Anglicans answer, in order to secure the validity of Parker's consecration. But that gives up the whole question; for if Barlow was a consecrated Bishop there was no need to take such extraordinary precautions in order to anticipate the objections which it was evidently expected would be made against the validity of Barlow's action.

Again, the original document gives the dates of consecration of Barlow's assistants, together with the names of their consecrators. Of Barlow, however, it can only say that "he was consecrated in the time of Henry VIII.," the registrar being unable to give any date, though he had access to official documents and could have consulted Barlow who was then living. In the official account, all reference to Barlow's having been consecrated at all is suppressed, the compilers evidently being of opinion that the less said about Barlow's consecration the better. Of course what Lingard observes is quite true that "it seems most unreasonable without direct proof" to suppose that Barlow remained unconsecrated; but direct proofs having come to light since Lingard's time, *presumptio cedit veritati*. The presumptive evidence in Barlow's favour is dealt with by Estcourt (p. 60) and Hutton (p. 303) and therefore the replies need not here be reproduced. But taking the evidence as it stands at present, it is as clearly proved as any negative proposition can be, that Barlow was never a consecrated Bishop.

J. D. BREEN.

Before and After Gunpowder Plot.

BY E. HEALY THOMPSON, M.A.

THIS famous plot for blowing up the Parliament House together with the King, Lords, and Commons assembled therein, which was fraught with such woeful consequences to the Catholics of England, and which even at this day. is used by their enemies as a polemical engine against them—as though it had been the work of the whole Catholic body, and had received the sanction of their ecclesiastical superiors—was, in fact, the secret conspiracy of a few individuals, mostly young men, whom the barbarous cruelties to which they and their families were subjected had driven to desperation, and, I may even say, goaded to madness.

Of the terrible penal laws which were designed to exterminate the ancient faith we may all have some idea, more or less definite. But it is only when we see them exemplified in individual cases, as recorded in the biographies of the sufferers or in the annals of the time, that we realize the true nature of the persecution which the Catholics of England had to endure on account of their religion: its bitterness, its brutality, its pitiless persistency, extending as it did to persons of both sexes of every rank and condition in life, young and old, rich and poor, the meanest equally with the noblest in the realm.

Many of the following particulars (supplemented from other sources) are taken from the *Life of Mary Ward*, which forms two volumes of the "Quarterly Series," published by Burns and Oates. Mary Ward was a member of one of the great Yorkshire families, of ancient lineage, and allied to many of the historic nobles of the land. Her history is extremely interesting, not only on account of her wonderful strength and energy of character, and the zeal she displayed in sustaining the faith and exciting the fervour of her oppressed and disheartened compatriots, especially by devoting herself to the education and training of girls of English parentage, whether for social or religious life; but from the fact of her having been among the first to form, not without much obloquy and opposition, an active association of women, unenclosed, which in her day was a novelty, and indeed, it may be said, an anomaly, in the Church. The institute took its rise in Flanders, and its members were known as the English Virgins; but of this I am not concerned to speak. I shall confine myself to a brief account of the penal enactments alluded to in her Life, and to the instances which she incidentally gives of the sufferings which some of her nearest relatives and friends underwent, simply because they refused to conform to the new religion which Henry VIII. and his daughter Elizabeth set up, and which they sought to maintain by laws of savage cruelty—laws which James I. determined to enforce with even greater rigour, in spite of the promises he had expressly made to his Catholic subjects on his accession to the throne of England. Viscount Montague, who, in 1604, stood up bravely in the House of Lords to oppose these persecuting enactments, was sent to prison for his speech.

For half a century the Catholics of England had been groaning under a tyranny to which the only parallel is to be found in the horrible treatment to which the early Christians were exposed under the heathen Emperors of Rome. The persecuting statutes had gone on increasing in severity, until the domestic misery they entailed was aggravated to a degree which no words can adequately describe. Some of the Catholic gentry, in despair of any mitigation of their sufferings, had gone to live abroad; but this mode of deliverance was not in the power of the far larger number even of the more opulent among them.

To these, therefore, nothing was left but the hard choice of violating their conscience by conforming to the laws, or incurring the loss of their whole property, imprisonment for life, or death; and, for what were esteemed minor offences, confinement for shorter periods and heavy fines, the frequent infliction of which reduced many to absolute beggary. Priests had no alternative. Death was the punishment assigned to them by law, although, as a matter of policy, this was in certain instances changed into imprisonment or banishment, while those who sheltered and assisted them were treated as felons: in other words, doomed to lifelong imprisonment or death. And what a death! In the *Middesex County Records*, vol. i., under September 18, 30th Elizabeth, we read the following decree respecting one William Hartley, a priest: "That he be drawn on a hurdle to the place of execution, and there be hung by the neck, whilst still alive be laid upon the ground, his members be amputated, his entrails be drawn out of his belly, *he being still alive*, and be burned, his head be cut off, and his body divided into four parts, and his head and quarters be placed where the Lady the Queen has been pleased to appoint."*

* In the record William Hartley is described as a "traitor," inasmuch as he had been "ordained a priest in parts beyond the sea by authority from the See of Rome, in contempt of the said Queen's crown and dignity, and also against the form of the statutes in this case published and provided." In fact, he was put to death simply and solely for being a priest and saying Mass. On this subject the historian Hallam, who cannot be suspected of unduly favouring Catholics, makes these just remarks: "Treason, by the law of England and according to the common use of language, is the crime of rebellion or conspiracy against the Government. If a statute is made by which the celebration of certain religious rites is subjected to the same penalties as rebellion, or conspiracy, would any man free from prejudice, and not designing to impose upon the uninformed, speak of persons convicted on such a statute as guilty of treason, without expressing in what sense he uses the words? . . . A man is punished for religion, when he incurs a penalty for its profession or exercise to which he was not liable on any other account. This is applicable to the great majority of capital convictions on this score under Elizabeth," and, it may be added, under James I. also. "The persons convicted could not be traitors in any fair sense of the word, because they were not chargeable with anything properly

Such was the punishment awarded to the priests and professors of the old religion. In 1596 and the two following years, the storm raged fiercely around York. Not only were the prisons crowded with recusants (as those were called who refused to acknowledge the Queen's spiritual supremacy), but eleven persons were executed for the faith, three being priests and eight laymen, both gentlemen and others. Two women, Anne Tesh and Bridget Maskew, were condemned to be burned "for persuading a minister to be a Catholic;" and, though reprieved, were left in prison until the accession of James I. Beside many others, Ralph Grimston, a connection of Mary Ward's, was condemned as a felon for assisting a priest, a native of Ripon, who was executed in 1598. Mary's father had to break up his household and leave the neighbourhood.

In the month of October, 1605, just before the discovery of the plot, two priests and a layman had suffered the extreme penalty of the law. They were executed together with sixteen thieves and eight other malefactors; and their heads were placed on London Bridge. Luisa de Carvajal, a Spanish lady of noble birth, who had come to England in the May of this same year with the heroic intention of succouring the persecuted Catholics, even at the risk of martyrdom, and who became acquainted with Mary Ward during one of the frequent visits which the latter made to this country, writes: "We can hardly go out to walk without seeing the heads and limbs of some of our dear and holy ones stuck up on the gates that divide the streets, and the birds of the air perching upon them; which makes me think of the verse in the Psalms, 'They have given the dead bodies of Thy servants to be meat for the fowls of the air, the flesh of Thy saints to the beasts of the earth.'" *

It was death to reconcile any one to the Catholic Church. To hear Mass, receive the Sacraments, educate children as Catholics, even to wear or possess rosaries,

denominated treason" (*Constitutional History* chap. iii n. pp. 164 165, edit. 1850).
* *Life of Luisa de Carvajal*, by Lady G. Fullerton, p. 226.

crosses, an *Agnus Dei*, and such like things blessed by the Pope, was punishable with loss of property or perpetual imprisonment; sometimes with both. In these same *Middlesex County Records*, December 8, 20th Elizabeth, we read of a certain Elinore Brome, wife of Sir Christopher Brome, late of Islington, having received from her sister, Lady Pawlett, a certain token called an *Agnus Dei*, brought into this kingdom of England from the See of Rome, with the intention of using the said token, and that she actually wore it about her neck—showing that she must have been searched in order to its discovery. She was convicted of felony, and was awarded the penalty of the statute. But, oppressive and sanguinary as were these laws, the King and his counsellors were not satisfied; and in 1604 a proclamation had been issued admonishing all magistrates and judges to be more rigorous in enforcing them: courts were held every six weeks whereat recusants were presented and condemned; houses were broken into at night under the pretence of searching for ecclesiastics.* The life of a Catholic who was faithful to his conscience was one of daily and constant alarm and solicitude. He was at the mercy of every ill-wisher or designing person; a discontented tenant, an evil-disposed servant, had him in their power; he was liable to be incessantly watched, and at any moment hurried off before the tribunals and condemned to heavy fines, imprisonment—well if it were not to death—on the most insufficient testimony.

But there were other cleverly contrived engines of oppression, which in themselves utterly destroyed the peace and well-being of the Catholic family, either rich or poor, one of which was a powerful aid in rooting up the Catholic religion and turning England into a Protestant country. This was the law which enforced attendance, baptism, and communion in Protestant churches. The penalty for disobedience was at first 12d. for each Sunday, but, as this was found ineffectual, in 1586 it was increased to £20 a month. Afterwards men

---

* Lingard, *History of England*, vol. ix., chap. i.

were made to pay £10 extra for their Catholic wives, and the same for their children; £10 also for their servants, thirteen months being reckoned in the year. James, indeed, at the end of the first year of his reign, exacted payment in full of all the fines incurred since his accession. Those who were unable to pay were deprived of two thirds of their goods; and under this statute the poor suffered terribly. Many went to prison rather than pay. It was a fine opportunity for the pursuivants and their underlings to gratify both their cruelty and their cupidity. We read of "coverlets and blankets taken from the beds" in the cottages—nay, the very beds themselves, and other furniture, even "the cloth which had been spun to clothe the children for winter." Sometimes all their goods were seized, the cow driven away, and the owners forced to go begging. On one occasion—I am still quoting the *Life of Mary Ward*—the vestry of a Protestant church was almost filled with pots, pans, pewter, and household stuff which had been carried off. On another, the milk on the fire, begged by a starving man in a cottage all but stripped, was poured away and the pan taken. These are but instances out of thousands such. How deep the faith still lay (adds the writer) in the hearts of the English poor may be seen by their simple but brave answers before their judges. Thus, in depositions taken at York in 1576, a tailor's wife "sayeth she cometh not to the church because there is neither altar nor sacrifice;" a locksmith, "because it is not the Catholic Church, for there is neither priest, altar, nor sacraments;" his wife, that "her conscience will not serve her, because there is not the Sacrament hung up, nor other things as hath been aforetime."* How large were the numbers of sufferers among the poor and lower classes is shown by the fact that, in a list of recusants refusing to go to church in 1605, out of just 2,000 named only 50 are of the rank of gentlemen. "In the county and city of York alone there were indicted in this same year 1,000 recusants; in Lancashire, 600; in the western

---

* *Recusant Papers*, under the date in the Public Record Office.

counties of Devon, Dorset, Cornwall, Somerset, Wilts, and Hants, 924; in six other counties, 700; in seven others, 923; in eight others, 1,865; in five others, 114; making together—and we have not enumerated all the counties of England, because we have not the statistics of all—the extraordinary total of 6,126. Can it be matter of wonder that, under the pressure of so severe and so universal a persecution, some among the proscribed should have had recourse to the most desperate remedies, even remedies involving the commission of great and grievous crimes?"*

"The recusants in the middle classes of life were ground to the dust by the repeated forfeiture of all their personal estates, with two-thirds of their lands and leases. These penalties were exacted with such rigour by the Bishops of Hereford and Llandaff, that in the county of Hereford alone 409 families suddenly found themselves reduced to a state of beggary. It required but little additional provocation to goad men in such extremity to acts of violence. To reduce the higher ranks to an equality with their more indigent brethren, the Bishops received orders, at the suggestion of the Chancellor, to excommunicate the opulent or more zealous Catholics within their dioceses, to certify the names into the Chancery, and to sue for writs, by which the delinquents would become liable to imprisonment and outlawry, incapable of recovering debts, or rents, or damages for injuries, of making sales or purchases, or of conveying their estates by deed or will. To add to their terrors, a report was spread that in the next Parliament measures would be adopted to ensure the total extirpation of the ancient faith; and the report seemed to be confirmed by the injurious epithets which the King in his daily conversation bestowed on the Catholics, by the menacing directions of the Chancellor in the Star-chamber, and by the hostile language of the Bishop

* *Clifton Tracts*, n. 50, p. 12; to which the reader is referred for fuller details of the persecution and of the causes which led to the Plot. He will there find the whole matter clearly and judiciously treated within the compass of a few pages.

of London in his sermon at St. Paul's Cross."* The State-bishops, it may be observed, were always foremost in the work of persecution.

Another ingenious plan King James devised for mulcting his Catholic subjects, which added insult to injury. In the year 1605, the very year of the Plot, but prior to its discovery, he began farming them out to his Scotch favourites, as greedy as they were needy. That is to say, making use of a power which had been given him, of refusing the £20 a month for recusancy and taking two-thirds of the whole property instead, he allowed these hungry dependents of his to choose for themselves a number of wealthy Catholics, and exact from them all the penalties to which they had become liable, or oblige them to make these Scotchmen an annuity for life in lieu of the immediate payment of the full sums which were due to the royal exchequer. Lists of the sufferers are still extant, as well as of the King's grasping followers to whom liberty was given "to make profit" of them. Among the former are the names of many well-known Catholic families, who have remained faithful to the cause of God and His Church.

The value of money being much greater than it is now,† few incomes would bear the penalty, the price at which the richer Catholics were to buy peace of conscience; and thus many of them were completely ruined. This was the case with Sir Ralph Babthorpe, whose daughter Barbara was the friend of Mary Ward's girlhood, and afterwards one of the first associates of her institute. Indeed, his house had been the shelter and chosen home of her youth. The Babthorpe family had become the objects of bitter persecution. In 1592 Grace Babthorpe, Sir Ralph's wife, had been sent to prison, after being examined before the Earl of Huntingdon, who was President of the North from 1572 to 1599. He first questioned her in private, and asked her when she had gone to the Protestant service? She answered him,

* Lingard, *History of England*, vol. ix., chap. i.
† Dr. Jessopp says, "roughly ten times" (*One Generation of Norfolk House*, pp. 203, 305, 316).

"Never." He then demanded how many Masses she had heard? So many, she replied, that she could not reckon them. At this he began to stamp, and the next day had her brought up before the whole Council-table at York, where himself and the Archbishop presided. She was committed to prison, and remained there two years. Matthews, the Protestant Archbishop, was especially hostile to Sir Ralph, and had caused his children to be baptized by a Protestant minister, though they had already been baptized by a Catholic priest. Citations, couched in the most odious terms, were issued against him monthly, or were publicly read in Protestant churches. After levying exorbitant fines upon him, the Archbishop, at length, by virtue of the statutes enacted by James I., seized on two-thirds of his estate; and, the one-third remaining being soon exhausted by further fines, he left the country and went to live at Louvain on the poor remnants of his fortune. Sir Ralph had been a man of very large property, possessing several mansions and a numerous body of retainers. It is said of him that he was "so well beloved for his bountiful and good disposition that he had not so much as one enemy;" but his fidelity to the faith reduced him to utter poverty, and he died with scarcely a servant to attend him in his old age.

But there was another intolerable outrage, to which I have as yet only incidentally alluded. In these evil days the home of a Catholic Englishman was certainly not his castle. At any hour of the day or night his house might be suddenly invaded by a magistrate at the head of an armed mob, or still worse, by pursuivants with a gang of attendants, notorious for being a most degraded, mercenary, unscrupulous, and cruel set of men, many of them apostates from the faith, who made a living by such means. The doors would be burst open, and the pursuivants would run up the stairs and into the chambers with drawn swords, "enough" (to use the words of a contemporary) "to drive the weaker sort of women and children out of their wits." Indeed, Mary Ward relates how on St. Luke's day, 1613, the constables broke into the house of her friend, Luisa de Carvajal, and found the lady praying with her companions, one of whom lay dangerously ill of small-pox, and another was nursing her. Within twenty-four hours the sick lady died of fright, deprived (she adds) of all the holy sacraments of the Church. These men, invested as they were with the authority of the law, would ransack every room, and search and interrogate every person at their will; turning men, women, and children out of their beds, if it were night, under the plea that superstitious objects might be hidden there; the tapestry would be torn down, the walls pierced, the flooring torn up, locks forced, closets, drawers, coffers rifled. Remonstrances only made them more insolent. They recklessly wasted and destroyed whatever was in their way, and finally would carry off private letters, plate, and anything valuable they found, besides whatever else they fancied, even beds, tables, clothes, chests, trunks, and especially money. "If they find the master of the house, they thrust the infamous oath of supremacy upon him; and, if he refuses to take it, they carry him off to the nearest gaol, there in poverty and chains, in darkness and squalor, in hunger and nakedness, to drag out his life or die. The times of Elizabeth" (concludes the writer), "although most cruel, were the mildest and happiest in comparison with those of James I."* "Not only in the shires and provinces" (writes another), "but in London itself, and under the eyes of the Court, the violence and insolency of continual searches grew to be intolerable; no night passing, commonly, but that soldiers and catchpoles broke into quiet men's houses when they were asleep, and not only carried their persons into prisons at their pleasure, unless they would bribe excessively, but whatsoever liked them best."†

Sometimes these inroads were directed against single houses or individuals; at other times they were sudden organized attacks upon all the Catholics throughout

---

* *Stonyhurst Manuscripts, Anglia*, vol. iii. n. p. 103.
† Parsons, *Judgment of a Catholic Englishman*, p. 43.

whole districts, and that on the slightest pretexts. Thus the Protestant Bishop of Hereford—and the Protestant Bishops, to their shame be it recorded, were among the fiercest persecutors—writes to Cecil, James's Minister, in June, 1605: "On Wednesday last, at evening, Sir James Scudamore and other justices of the peace, with such aid as I could give them, went unto the Darren and other places adjoining to make search and apprehend Jesuits and priests . . . and did make diligent search all that night and day following, from village to village, from house to house, about thirty miles compass, near the confines of Monmouthshire, where they found altars, images, books of superstition, relics of idolatry, but left all desolate of men and women. Except here and there an aged woman or a child, all were fled into Wales, and but one man apprehended; all that circuit of rude barbarous people carried headlong into these desperate courses by priests (whereof there is great store) and principal gentlemen, lords of towns and manors there. They are all fled into woods, and there they will lurk until the assizes be past." Such is the language which this false prelate uses towards the adherents of the old religion, and the manner in which he hounds on the pursuivants to their destruction. Father Holtby, speaking of a similar hunt in search of Catholics all over Yorkshire and other neighbouring counties on February 1, 1593, relates how all the justices of the peace and others in authority, together with a host of Protestant ministers, entered the houses of the Catholics in so great numbers that it was hard to say how many were abroad that night in searching. "There came," he says, "to some houses above a hundred or seven score persons to search. Myself and my brother John escaped very narrowly. They got beads and books in divers places, and many were forced to forsake their homes to escape the danger; yet did they also seek the grounds and woods in many places. A few laymen were taken, and one only priest."* "This hunting for Catholics" (aptly observes

---

* *Father Holtby's Narrative*, given by Father Morris in his *Troubles of our Catholic Forefathers*, vol. iii. p. 164.

the biographer of Mary Ward) "might be the description of an unsuccessful *battue* for game when the country assembles for sport, and little results except the destruction of a few hares and pheasants. It was a continually renewed excitement, especially for the idle and ill-disposed portion of the population, of which the poor unoffending Catholic was the victim. To him the consequences were not trifling." The closest retirement, the most obscure position, did not suffice to protect him, and whichever way he looked there seemed no earthly hope. "Catholics" (writes Dona Luisa, p. 225) "never have a moment of peace and security, or hear a noise at the door without a beating of the heart, especially if they have a priest residing with them.* Numbers of people answer me when I speak to them of religion, 'We have not the least doubt that the Catholic religion is the true one, but how is it possible to exist in such continual fear and trembling; not to be able, whether in bed or at meals, in the house or out of it, to enjoy the least tranquillity?' And thus, driven to despair, they risk, or rather forfeit, their hopes of salvation."

In the *Life of Mary Ward* we have instances of the manner in which some of her own relatives were treated by the pursuivants. Thus, in 1586, or 1587, the Lord President Huntingdon went at night to the house of Mrs. Ardington, of Harewell, together with certain "bad companions of his household." Entering the room in which Dame Isabel Whitehead, a nun of the Benedictine Priory of Arthington—dissolved in 1540, and granted to Archbishop Cranmer for his youngest son— lay sick in bed, they stood over her with their naked swords and rapiers, and threatened to kill her unless she would tell them where David Ingleby and Mr. Winsour, Mrs.

---

* Many an old English mansion has enclosed within the thickness of its walls a low and narrow cell, which was once the hiding-place of some devoted priest, who carried his life in his hands, liable at any moment to be seized and hurried away to torture and to death; and many a thrilling story of sudden arrest or hairbreadth escape is to be found in Challoner's *Missionary Priests*, or in that marvel of labour and industry, *Jesuit Records*, collected from the archives of the Society and the annals of our old Catholic families, by Henry Foley, S.J., in 8 vols., demy 8vo, of 700 pages each.

Ardington's brother and son-in-law, were. They then searched, rifled, turned and tossed all things upside down, but found nothing to their purpose, except some doublets, hose, and silk and guernsey stockings, belonging to a gentleman, which they forthwith appropriated. After staying some days in the house, and living at free quarters, they carried off Mrs. Ardington, together with the sick nun and other women, and committed them close prisoners in York and others places.

Imprisonment in those days was a very different matter from what it is now. The condition of the prisons was horrible; numbers of Catholics died in them, some after a year or more, others lingering for periods of eight, ten, twelve, even twenty years, and finally sinking under their sufferings. It was not only the dungeons of the Tower, or the lower wards of the Gatehouse, Counter, Clink, and other London prisons, where criminals were thrust into a hole, with only straw for their bed, and no other light but a candle, and where the inmates died from the filth and infection, although they paid for ordinary lodging: the gaols in the country were as bad or even worse. We read of "filthy prisons full of vermin," and of "women remaining twenty weeks in a prison where they could not see at noonday to eat their meat without a candle, their beds loathsome with filth. In York Castle the prisoners became grievously diseased through the infectious air." The low Kidcote, Ousebridge, to which Mrs. Dorothy Vavasour, a lady of high family, was removed "after living virtuously many years in prison," is described as a "strait and pestilential place, where she and many others fell sick, and contracted such diseases as never left them until their dying day."* Out of fifty-eight persons who were incarcerated at York in the time of Archbishop Matthews, for refusing the "oath of allegiance,"† forty died in prison.

* "Notes by a prisoner in Ousebridge," quoted in the *Life of Mary Ward*, vol. i. p. 82.
† This oath, which was formulated by James I., in 1606, with the object of catching Catholics in its toils, and which, in fact, was the occasion of much dissension and prevarication among them,

A few extracts from the personal narratives of the sufferers will help us to realize the unspeakable horrors of these hells upon earth.

Richard Fulwood, who was servant to Father John Gerard, and helped him in effecting his wonderful escape from the Tower in 1597, writing to his master from the prison of Bridewell, in Holy Week, 1594, says that "he had hardly enough black bread to keep him from starving. His abode was a narrow, strongly-built cell, in which there was no bed, so that he had to sleep sitting on the window-sill, and was months without taking off his clothes. There was a little straw in the place, but it was so trodden down and swarming with vermin that he could not lie upon it. Besides all this, he was awaiting an examination by torture."* Father Gerard himself, speaking of the prison called the Counter, says, "I was thrust through a little narrow door into a cell under the roof, where there was nothing but a bed, and no room to stand upright, except just where the bed was. There was one window, open day and night, through which the foul air entered, and the rain fell on to my bed. The room door was so low that I had to enter, not on my feet, but on my knees, and even then I was forced to stoop. However, I reckoned this rather an advantage, inasmuch as it helped to keep out the strong and pestilential stench that came from the common place close to my door that was used by the prisoners in that part of the gaol. I was often kept awake by the bad smell, to say nothing of the injury to my health." Again, Father William Weston, describing his sufferings in Wisbeach Castle, says that "the terrible stench of the prison exceeded all its other miseries, and that he was so suffocated by its pestilential vapours that his natural feelings inclined him to wish for death. He could get no sleep unless his body, worn out by weakness, sank prostrate on the ground; and that, were he to reckon

was pressed upon all, men and women, above the age of eighteen. It was condemned by the Holy See, "as containing matters contrary to faith and salvation."

* *Jesuit Records*, vol. i. p. 494.

the time, he did not get more than ten hours' repose out of the fifty nights he spent there. He had only such wretched light as a narrow little window, like the loophole of a tower, afforded him; so that he esteemed it a blessing that he was not deprived of both sight and mind, although, as it was, his strength and head were so exhausted that he was unable either to write or read four lines consecutively. This castle was half in ruins, and had for a long time been abandoned and forgotten till it occurred to the ministers of Elizabeth to prepare it as a fitting place to despatch their victims by a lingering death in its pestilential atmosphere"—for it was situated in a fetid marshy place—"and so save themselves the odium entailed by the crying injustice of so many public executions."* And these, be it remembered, were holy servants of God, beloved and venerated for their piety and virtues, who, in the face of torments and death, were labouring for the salvation of souls; men, too, who, as Dr. Jessopp has said of Father Henry Walpole, executed at York, April 17, 1595, were "gentlemen of birth and fortune, men of exceptionally high culture, and of great intellectual gifts," who had sacrificed everything that the world most prizes in the interests of Divine truth.†

Further, the inmates of these loathsome prisons were dependent on the charity of the faithful for their food and sustenance; and even thus they were at the mercy of rapacious gaolers, who enriched themselves by starving their prisoners. More than this: in Wisbeach Castle they were chargeable with the diet and other necessaries of the Protestant minister appointed as chaplain to the

* *Ibid.* vol. ii. pp. 179, 180, 593.
† "Letters of Henry Walpole," quoted in *Jesuit Records*, vol. ii. p. 270. Dr. Jessopp subsequently wrote the history of Father Walpole in the volume already alluded to. As a Protestant, he could not be expected to appreciate at their true value the exalted aims of a "missionary priest;" but his work is remarkable for its minute and accurate research, its fearless honesty of purpose, its generous sympathy with the persecuted and detestation of the cruelties to which they were subjected. Father Walpole was repeatedly tortured before his martyrdom.

gaol, whose preaching they were required to attend, at least, twice in the week; if they refused, they were to be fined at the pleasure of the Bishop of Ely.* An instance is recorded of a gaoler, in whose breast pity was not utterly extinct, going to Aylmer, Bishop of London, and representing to him the extreme hunger and starvation from which his prisoners were suffering. He was angrily answered, "It is enough to feed them with bread and water." "Yes," said the gaoler, "but who will pay me for the bread? the water I will give with pleasure on my own account, but not a scrap of bread." To which this pious and charitable prelate, in a still greater rage, replied, "Get away! what do I care? Let the Papists eat their own excrements if they will."† These are the Right Reverend Fathers in God, who were forced upon the English people in place of the true Shepherds and Bishops of their souls; these are the men whom a newly-risen party in the Establishment would fain persuade us to recognise as the successors and representatives of the hierarchy of the old English Church—which certainly they themselves never affected to be, any more than the "ministers" under them pretended to be Mass-saying priests, commissioned to offer the Adorable Sacrifice: on the contrary, having thrown down the altars throughout the land, they blasphemously denounced and derided it as a Popish and idolatrous rite.

If the bare recital of these brutalities is enough to make one's blood boil with indignation, what must have been the feelings of high-spirited Englishmen, when they saw their dearest relatives—their mothers and wives, sisters and daughters—refined and cultured women, delivered into the hands of men so coarse and cruel, and consigned, it might be for years, to such dens of filth and misery? Mary Ward relates that her grandmother, while yet a young woman, had suffered imprisonment for the space of fourteen years together; and once, because in her examinations before the Lord President she had spoken in exaltation of the Catholic

---

* *Jesuits in Conflict*, p. 68.   † *Jesuit Records*, vol. ii. p. 635.

religion and contempt of heresy, she was thrust into a common prison or dungeon amongst thieves and other malefactors. On her entrance, the criminals there confined, judging that she had been committed for theft or murder (for such were all that came into that cave) told her she must contribute sixpence, as was the custom, to the common purse, or else she should not eat of their common meat, which was what good people of charity would give: all sorts of meats put together and so given in at the prison door. To this her grandmother willingly consented, and gave her sixpence. However, she stayed not long in this horrible pit, as, the matter being much spoken of, her kindred were able to procure her removal to the Castle prison, where she was before.*

This same Lord President imprisoned all the gentlewomen he could lay hold of—many of them more or less nearly related to Mary Ward—some in one castle, some in another, and locked them up apart in several wide chambers, so that they could not see or speak with each other, nor have any maid to wait upon them save such as was deputed for them by their gaolers. It would take long to tell what shifts they were put to, and what miseries they endured. In York prison there were at one time no fewer than fifty prisoners, of whom almost thirty were condemned to lose all their temporal goods and be incarcerated for life, for refusing the oath of allegiance, and also to death. Their necessities were often so great, living all in common at a common table of that which in charity was sent them, that they had no more for everyone than was according to the rate of a penny a day.†

Susanna Rookwood, daughter of Edward Rookwood, of Euston Hall, in Suffolk—whom Queen Elizabeth, when she visited him, caused to be committed to the town prison at Norwich for recusancy, where he remained for more than twenty years—was five times in prison

* *Life of Mary Ward*, vol. i. pp. 12, 13.
† F. Pollard's *Recollections of the Yorkshire Missions*, quoted in the *Life of Mary Ward*.

for her religion. Being one of Mary Ward's associates, she encouraged and refreshed the other prisoners both by spiritual and temporal means. At last she was thrown into a horrible dungeon, or rather hole, where she had to defend and preserve herself with a stick from the mice, rats, and other vermin which infested it. Here she was kept for a considerable time, but was at last set free, and, nothing discouraged by her sufferings, continued her pious labours for many years.

Mary Ward herself was cast into prison more than once. Abbot, Archbishop of Canterbury, who was a fanatical persecutor of the Catholics, issued a mandate for her apprehension, and, in order that she might not escape, published a precise description of her person. This was in 1617, and, yielding to the urgent entreaties of her friends, she left the country for a while, but returned the following year. This year, 1618–19, was one of great activity in England against the professors of the old religion, and both sexes had to bear the brunt of the conflict. The firm and faithful persistence of the women in Catholic families had drawn down upon them the especial animosity of the persecutors, and became a new source of enriching the ever needy Sovereign and his grasping courtiers. It was a year of heavy fines and exactions. All conforming husbands, that is, all who went occasionally to the Protestant church, were fined £220 a year—worth near upon £2,000 now—"till such time as they could persuade their wives to abjure their faith," and the wife had to go to prison if the husband did not pay. Mary Ward and her companions had made themselves particularly obnoxious by their labours and successes in reclaiming many to the faith, and were counted worthy of being strictly watched and hunted after; and here I may relate an instance of Mary's courage—I might even say audacity—which has a spice of humour in it. Learning that Abbot had a great curiosity to see her, she resolved to gratify it, in the hopes of softening his heart towards Catholics; attiring herself, accordingly, as a lady of quality (which in fact she was), she repaired, with some of her associates similarly dressed, to his palace at Lambeth, but, not finding his Grace at home, she—did not leave her card, as she might have done in these our days, but—with a diamond, wrote her name on a glass window in the hall.

The Archbishop ungraciously responded by issuing stricter orders to his myrmidons, who at length succeeded in capturing her, owing to the vessel in which she was embarked being turned back by a contrary wind. The prison to which she was taken was probably that of the Gatehouse at Westminster, as the warrants for her arrest had been sent out by Abbot. Women had been hanged during the persecution for less offences than that of Mary, and many there were who had died in prison, or were even then lingering in the miseries of a long captivity. Sentence of death was, in fact, passed upon her, almost without trial or the evidence of witnesses, as was frequently the case. But, after lying sometime in durance vile, she regained her liberty with the help of a golden key; a heavy price being offered by her friends and accepted by her gaolers, including his Grace of Canterbury.

Mention has been made of torture, a practice in respect to Catholics which certain Protestants have had the hardihood to deny, but of which there cannot remain the smallest doubt.* I might cite the notorious case of Father Gerard, who was put to the rack in the Tower three times, being "thrice hanged up by the hands, every time until he was almost dead, and that in one day twice;"† but I will give other examples, which I have lighted upon in the early volumes of Brother Foley's work. On December 10, 1580, "the blessed martyr, Father Cottam, underwent the torture called by the name of the 'Scavenger's Daughter' for the space of upwards of one hour, which caused him to bleed profusely from the nostrils. This terrible engine of torture was of very common use in the Tower. It was a broad iron

* Hallam, *Constitutional History*, chap. iii. pp. 140—142, edit. 1850.
† Morris, *Life of Father John Gerard*, Chap. xix.

hoop, consisting of two parts fastened to each other by a hinge. The sufferer was made to kneel on the pavement, and to contract himself into as small a compass as he could. Then the executioner, kneeling on his shoulders and having introduced the hoop under his legs, compressed the victim close together until he was able to fasten the extremities of the hoop over the small of the back. The time allotted to this kind of torture was one hour and a half, during which it commonly happened that, from excess of compression, the blood started from the nostrils, sometimes from the extremities of the hands and feet." On May 18, 1582, Father Cottam, in conjunction with three other priests, was executed at Tyburn under circumstances of peculiar cruelty and horror.

We left Father Gerard's servant, Richard Fulwood, "awaiting examination by torture." It was not long delayed. He suffered together with one called Little John, who had been taken to the Tower at the same time as Father Gerard himself. Unable either by coaxing or bribing to draw anything from them that could compromise others, the persecutors had recourse to threats and then to force. "They were both hung up for three hours together, having their arms fixed into iron rings and their bodies hanging in the air; a torture which causes frightful pain and intolerable extension of the sinews. It was all to no purpose; no disclosure could be wrested from them that was hurtful to others." This was in 1594; and in the same year, Father John Percy being seized by some English soldiers at Flushing, "they hung him up by the hands, and then tortured him by twisting a sail rope about his head. During the torture he fixed his mind on the eternity of either pain or joy, uttering no cry but 'O Eternity!' He was taken to London in custody and committed to Bridewell, where his cell consisted of an entirely unfurnished turret. His bed was the brick floor with a little straw over it." This act of torturing may be regarded as a sort of amateur proceeding on the part of some brutal soldiers, but not so the following, which took place by due course of law. At Bewdley, near Worcester, in 1584, a priest named Bennett, together with four laymen whom he was suspected of having reconciled to the Church, were put to the torture by order of the Judges, Bromley and Townsend. "They were suspended by the arms, *with heavy chains attached*, until they swooned, upon which they were let down, and their temples were washed with brandy until consciousness returned, when they were again hung up; and this was continued for several days. About the same time, a priest named Henry Bell, seventy years of age, was put to death, together with Henry Finch, a layman, for denying that the Queen was head of the Church. As Finch was the younger and bolder of the two, and openly contemned their prayers and sermons, they dragged him, more than once, by the heels and with his head knocking against the ground, so that he was all covered with blood," to their Protestant preachings; after which they hanged and quartered them as traitors.*

Not content, however, with inflicting bodily tortures on their victims, these agents of Satan laid snares also against their souls. Brother Foley mentions three instances in which women of impure life were introduced into the cells of the prisoners in the hope of enticing them to sin, so as to have occasion of fresh charges against them; one being an aged prelate of Mary's reign, Dr. Watson, Bishop of Lincoln, who had been long incarcerated and cruelly tortured.†

But enough of these ghastly details. I have given them simply in order to exhibit the terrible nature of the persecution to which the Catholics of England were

---

* *Jesuit Records*, vol. i. pp. 495, 523, 636, 637; vol. ii. pp. 159, 170–6. Father Bennett, "after an apostolical life of labour and suffering, died in London, a martyr of charity in attending the plague-stricken, at the age of seventy-five, in the year 1625."

† *Jesuit Records*, vol. ii. p. 162.

subjected on account of their fidelity to their religion, and the state of intolerable wretchedness to which they were reduced prior to the Gunpowder Plot, which, but for these infamous atrocities, would never have been contrived.

On this subject I cannot do better than adopt the following observations of Lady G. Fullerton, in her *Life of Luisa de Carvajal*,* which are as forcible as they are just. After speaking of the "horrible persecution, the maddening oppression and refinements of cruelty, which drove a few men wild with despair to plan the sudden destruction of a King and of a Parliament which were heaping upon Catholics the direst sufferings, and imperilling the souls of their children by the prohibition of Catholic worship and education," this admirable writer thus proceeds: "The sight of continual outrages, perpetrated under the name of law, worked like madness in their minds, and, oblivious of the Divine command not to do evil that good may come, they deemed it justifiable to use any means, however terrible, to deliver their brethren from a King who publicly drank 'damnation to the Papists'—one whose mother had died on the scaffold, consoled and strengthened in her mortal agony by the Catholic Faith—and from law-givers who placed them and their co-religionists beyond the pale of the law,† tortured and slew their priests, seduced their

---

* Pp. 157, 158.
† Sir Edward Hoby, a Protestant gentleman then residing in London, writes to Sir Thomas Esmonde: "My Lord Salisbury showed me a paper in the King's own hand, under the name of his *Meditations*, which you would have said was an Act of Parliament, the form only wanting: 'All recusants, convict, and not communicating [*i.e.* not taking the so-called sacrament in the Protestant Church] shall stand in the case of excommunicate persons, whereby they are clean out of the King's protection, subject to many dangers, and, upon any injury offered, not plead in any of the King's courts. The King to choose whether he will take £20 a month or two parts of their living. All women to be incapable of their dowers or jointures.'" Such were the godly "meditations" of "that sanctified person" (*Dedication of the Protestant Bible*) James I., which, as we shall see, he was subsequently able to put in execution.

children from the Faith, insulted and imprisoned their wives, invaded their homes, ruined their fortunes, confiscated their lands, and trod their rights under foot, and that for no other offence than worshipping God as every Christian had worshipped God for fifteen hundred years. No wonder that, yielding to human passion, they conceived the thought of swiftly and suddenly destroying the destroyers, forgetting Who has said, '*Vengeance is Mine, and I will repay!*' If extenuating circumstances can ever be pleaded for a great crime, the Gunpowder Plot may claim the benefit. Who shall dare to say that it exceeded the sin of the rulers who provoked it, or that the maddened victim does not deserve more mercy than the cold-blooded tyrant and ruthless oppressor? Be that as it may, they sinned, and they suffered, and all the Catholics of England suffered redoubled persecution through their guilty act. Fear made their enemies savage. The most sanguinary laws were passed, and all the fury of popular passion was let loose against them."

By these new enactments, says Lingard, "Catholic recusants were forbidden, under particular penalties, to appear at Court, to dwell within the boundaries, or ten miles of the boundaries, of the City of London, or to remove on any occasion more than five miles from their homes without a special license under the signatures of four neighbouring magistrates. 2. They were made incapable of practising in surgery or physic, or in the common or civil law; of acting as judges, clerks, or officers in any court or corporation; of presenting to the livings, schools, or hospitals in their gifts; or of performing the offices of administrators, executors, or guardians. 3. Husbands and wives, unless they had been married by a Protestant minister, were made to forfeit every benefit to which he or she might otherwise be entitled from the property of the other; unless their children were baptized by a Protestant minister within a month after the birth, each omission subjected them to a fine of £100; and, if after death they were not buried in a Protestant cemetery, their executors were liable to pay for each corpse the sum of £20.   4. Every child sent for education beyond the sea was from that moment debarred from taking any benefit by devise, descent, or gift, until he should return and conform to the Established Church, all such benefit being assigned by law to the Protestant next of kin.   5. Every recusant was placed in the same situation as if he had been excommunicated by name; his house might be searched, his books and furniture having, or thought to have, any relation to his worship or religion, might be burned, and his horses and arms might be taken from him at any time by order of the neighbouring magistrates.   6. All the existing penalties for absence from church were continued, but with two amendments: it was made optional in the King whether he would take the fine of £20 per lunar month, or in lieu of it all the personal and two-thirds of the real estate; and every householder, of whatever religion, receiving Catholic visitors or keeping Catholic servants, was liable to pay for each individual £10 per lunar month.   7. A new oath was devised, all who refused to take it being subjected to perpetual imprisonment and the forfeiture of their personal property and of the rents of their lands during life: or, if they were married women, to imprisonment in the common gaol, until they should repent of their obstinacy and submit to take the oath." This is the oath still taken by the Anglican clergy.

189:

OR

The Church of Old England protests.

BY THE

REV. J. D. BREEN, O.S.B.

THOSE who claim the title of "Defenders" of the Anglican Establishment have repeated with much assurance the assertion that the Church of England reformed herself in Elizabeth's time, and that only 189 of the old clergy refused to conform. Such an important statement of alleged facts invites criticism. Queen Mary died Nov. 17th, 1558. Elizabeth soon made known her intended policy by her first measures. Cecil, Becon, Parr, Russell, Earl Dudley and Sadler, all Protestants, and Lord Howard, Sir. R. Sackville, the Earl of Arundel, and Paulet, Marquis of Winchester, professed Catholics, were summoned to the Council. Whyte, bishop of Winchester, was imprisoned for his sermon at Mary's funeral, and the clergy were forbidden for the present to preach. These measures seriously alarmed the bishops of the Church of England. The bench was constituted as follows: Ten of the sees, including Canterbury, were vacant by death; Nicholas *Heath* was Archbishop of York, and, during the vacancy of Canterbury, head of the Church of England; *Tunstall* was bishop of Durham, Whyte of Winchester, *Bonner* of London, *Thirlby* of Chester, *Day* of Chichester, Turberville of Exeter, Bourne of Bath and Wells, *Poole* of

Peterborough, Bayne of Lichfield, Oglethorpe of Carlisle, Goldwell of St. Asaph's, Kitchin of Llandaff, Scott of Chester, Watson of Lincoln, *Pate* of Worcester.* The bishop of Man had been deprived already.

The bishops met to consider the situation, and, seeing that the Queen evidently intended not to keep the oaths she would have to take, resolved that they would take no part in her coronation and in the profanity of helping her to perjure herself. This may be considered the *first* protest of the Church of England in the person of her bishops against the proposed change of religion. Oglethorpe was finally prevailed on to perform the coronation ceremony, on the express condition that the queen should take the usual oath to maintain the Catholic faith and receive Communion under one kind according to the Roman ritual.

The Acts of Uniformity and Supremacy were then prepared to present to the coming Parliament. The Prayer-book was revised by a Commission, all Protestants. In those days it was an easy matter to get a House of Commons pledged to pass any measures proposed by the crown. Lists of the persons to be returned were sent to the sheriff, and these were returned accordingly, for the ministers had good reason to fear any *free* expression of opinion on the part of the English people in matters of religion. In the House of Lords a stout resistance to the proposed measures was expected, and steps were taken to meet it. Two bishops were imprisoned, four others were not allowed to take their seats, and five Protestant peers were created in order to vote for the bills, thus making a difference of eleven votes. The Earl of Arundel and Duke of Norfolk, the natural leaders of the opposition, were gained over

---

* Those named in italics were bishops before Mary's time. Five bishops deposed by Cranmer were restored to their Sees by Mary and their deposition Hallam admits to have been wholly unjustifiable.

one by a promise to marry the Queen and the other by a promise of a nuptial dispensation he was anxious to obtain. The rest of the peers were promised that if they would only pass the bills they would personally be exempt from taking the Oath of Supremacy. And thus a majority of three was obtained, clearly proving that had there been such a thing as a *free* Parliament these bills would have been rejected by a considerable majority.

In the House of Commons, too, in spite of its having been packed, the opposition was so strong that it was only by a *ruse* that the Supremacy Bill was carried. "The Supremacy Bill went back to a Committee ; a week later it was reintroduced, slightly, though not materially, altered ; and again the opposition was so violent that it would have been lost except for Cecil, who, in De Feria's words, 'flung the question into a garboyle,' and carried his point in the confusion" (Froude, Hist. of England, vi., p. 163).

While these measures were under discussion, the clergy met in Convocation and drew up, January 24, a solemn declaration of their adherence to the Catholic faith in five Articles which included (1) the Real Presence, (2) Transubstantiation, (3) the Sacrifice of the Mass, (4) Supremacy of the Pope, and (5) denying the right of laymen to rule the Church.* They were accepted by the bishops and presented to the Government only to be ignored. They constitute, however, the *second* protest of the Church of England, as represented by her bishops and clergy lawfully assembled in Convocation against the new Anglican system. Froude points out that this was the protest of the whole *spiritualty* of England, and adds :—"And yet we are told that the Church of England reformed herself,—meaning by the Church not the laity, who alone did the work, but the bishops and

---

* See Dodd, vol. II. Appendix xxxix. Also 'Anglican Jurisdiction : is it Valid?' by J. D. Breen, O.S.B., p. 46.

clergy, who never consented, as a body, to any measure of reformation whatever, except under the judicious compulsion of Henry the Eighth" (Hist. of England, vi. p. 165).

Not only so, but Archbishop Heath, as head of the Church of England, spoke strongly against the proposed bill in the House of Lords, March 22, 1559. Strype gives a summary of the speech. He says:—"Heath spoke of two points:—the former that by this act they must forsake the See of Rome and the weight and force, danger and inconvenience thereof; and the latter, to consider what this supremacy to be given to the Queen was . . . . As to the first, he said that by forsaking and fleeing from the See of Rome they must first forsake and flee from all General Councils; secondly, all canonical and ecclesiastical law; thirdly, the judgment of all other Christian princes; and fourthly, the *unity* of Christ's Church, and by falling out of Peter's ship, hazard themselves to be drowned in the waters of schisms, sects and divisions, &c., &c."* Protest number *three*.

When it came to a division *all* the bishops present voted against any change in religion. Protest number *four*.

On the 15th of May, the bishops were summoned to meet the Queen at Greenwich, when she told them that it was her pleasure that they should either take the new Oath of Supremacy or resign their sees. The Archbishop, in the name of the Church of England, bade her "remember what her real duty was and the policy she was bound to adopt," "to follow in the steps of her sister who had brought back the country to the ancient religion, which had flourished in it for so many centuries;" that Rome was the mother of all Churches; that history and tradition, and the writings of the fathers and the great Councils of the Church all proclaimed Rome as the Head of that Church which their Divine Master had founded, &c., &c. Protest number *five*.

---

* Also Dodd, vol. ii. xxxv.

The twenty-one days' grace allowed within which to take the oath having elapsed, the bishops were arrested like common felons and thrust into the Tower and the Fleet, and finally were *all* deprived of their sees, except Kitchin. Protest number *six*.

As the bishops form the executive of the Church, too much stress cannot be laid upon these facts when Church Defenders tell us that the change of religion in this reign was the doing of the Church of England herself.

The Government was placed thus in a position of considerable embarrassment. The deprived bishops would of course never consent to consecrate intruders into their own sees, and they only could legally do so. On 18th of July, 1559, a *congé d'elire* was issued to the dean and chapter of Canterbury to elect Parker archbishop. Only four of the canons would have anything to do with his election. They pronounced the rest contumacious, and left the matter in the hands of Dean Wotton, a man of "both gospels." He of course named Parker, who of course accepted "lest he should seem to resist the divine will," etc.* This was the first flaw in the proceeding: Parker was never canonically elected. The next step was more serious. How was he to procure consecration? By the statute 25 of Henry VIII, an archbishop and two bishops, or else *four* bishops holding office in the Church of England, must officiate to make a consecration legal, and by the law of the Church *three* bishops, acting with the consent of the rest of the bench. On 9th September, a precept was issued to Tunstall of Durham, Bourne of Bath and Wells, Poole of Peterborough, and Kitchin of Landaff, also to Barlow and Scory, ordering them to confirm and consecrate Parker, and to perform all things necessary according to the laws and customs of the realm.† The first three had not as

* Strype's Parker, 52, 53.
† Rymer, xv. 541.

yet been actually deprived, probably in view of the present contingency. Had they been willing to act with Kitchin, using the consecration service of the old Church of England, there would be no ground to question the legality or validity of Parker's consecration.

To their eternal honour be it said, they refused to have anything to do with Parker's appointment, and were in consequence deprived. To ask them to consecrate as archbishop a man who was openly cohabiting with a person to whom he was not and could not be married by any law of Church or State was an insult to the whole bench; and to associate them with two degraded clerics, like Barlow and Scory, was a further insult, which they were bound to resent. This was the *last* and *final* protest of the English bishops against the establishment of Anglicanism.

On 6 December, a fresh precept was issued to Barlow, Scory, Coverdale and Hodgkins, and three others. The four first proceeded to act. They were broken-down friars, who had incurred excommunication by the law and practice of the Church of England for incontinence. Not one was holding any office in the Church of England. Hodgkins had been only suffragan of Bedford; Scory who had resigned, and Coverdale, were in the same boat with Taylor, Hooper, etc., who had been deprived in Mary's reign on account of the nullity of their consecration, and Barlow had also resigned, and the fact that he was ever a consecrated bishop has had to be assumed, for it cannot be proved. They had no more claim to act in the name of the Church of England than in that of one of the choirs of angels. A consciousness of radical defect in this process from the very beginning is evident from the fact that the Queen undertook to supply by her supreme royal authority every defect in the manner of their proceeding or in the quality, status or power of all or any of them or in any point presented by the laws of the Church or State, the circumstance of the time and the necessity of the case so requiring; a clause inserted for six years in every appointment of a bishop.* Not only so : Parker is said to have been consecrated by Cranmer's ordinal, which had been declared in Mary's reign illegal as well as invalid, when some of those in whose consecration it had been used had been deprived on the express ground of the nullity of their consecration.

Parker having thus illegally and sacrilegiously obtained the position of primate, proceeded to fill up the vacant sees with reformers, who were all Calvinists except Cheney of Gloucester, a Lutheran. A greater outrage against the rights and liberties of the Church of England was never committed. The whole bench of bishops except one, was deposed by a council of laymen, without being even charged with any offence that would entail their deprivation according to the law of the Church of England.† Men were thrust into their places who were not even members of the Church of England. They had been such, but had publicly and formally left her to join the sects of Calvin and Luther, sects which had as little in common with the old Church as the Salvation Army has with the present Establishment. Moreover, as long as a bishop lives and is not deprived of his see by the ordinary process of canonical law, no one else can, *in facie Ecclesiæ*, lawfully take possession of it. The claim to ownership is barred: there is another in possession. "He that entereth not by the door into the sheepfold but climbeth up some other way, the same is a thief and a robber,"‡ are the words of Christ: and yet Church Defenders are forced by the exigencies of their position to maintain that it was the old English bishops and not these Calvinist and Lutheran preachers who were the schismatics and intruders!

The illegality of the position of these intruders on the

---

* "Anglican Orders: are they Valid?" by J. D. Breen, O.S.B., p. 54.
† The refusal to take the Oath of Supremacy was merely a civil offence.   ‡ St. John x. i.

ground even of civil, as well as of ecclesiastical, law, was fully established in 1565. Bonner challenged the fact that they were bishops, even such as the law required, and the bench held that his plea was good in law. An Act had to be passed to make good by the *authority of Parliament* all that had been done in constituting the new hierarchy, *anything to the contrary notwithstanding*.

Seeing, then, that the bishops of the Church of England refused to hand on the succession to Parker, or to admit him to the episcopacy, and that the only right he and his following had to their positions rested upon this Act, they were known henceforth as *Parliamentary* bishops, and such have they been considered ever since.

If it be within the power of Parliament to unmake and make a bench of bishops, "anything to the contrary notwithstanding," there is no more to be said, but most Christians hold that it has no more power to do so than it has to make or unmake a solar system.

It will be a happy day for the descendants of these intruders when they are able to shake themselves loose from the incubus of the royal supremacy, this fossilized relic of Tudor tyranny and the divine right of kings. It is a principle which makes the whole Anglican system a bye-word and reproach amongst Christian believers, for it places practically in the hands of the head of the ministry, who may be a sceptic or infidel, the appointment of all its bishops; and in the hands of a council, who may be all unbelievers, the settlement of all appeals "like as in cases of appeal from the admiral's court," from the archbishop's court even in matters of faith and discipline. It will be a red letter day for our separated brethren when they can say, even at the cost of half their possessions, "the snare is broken and we are free."

So much as to the position assumed by the bishops. The attitude of the lower clergy will be equally clear from the following facts:—

On May 23, 1559, a commission was issued to visitors to tender the Oath of Supremacy to the clergy. They had orders not to push anyone to extremities on account of his oath, and thus their hands were tied.

The nature of the reception which the proposed change of religion was expected to meet with from the clergy may be gathered from the "Device for the alteration of religion," drawn up by the secret council whose members were Parker, Bill, May, Cox, Grindal, Whitehead and Pilkington, under Sir Thomas Smith. One of the obstacles to be dealt with was: "Bishops and all the clergy will see their ruin. In confession, preaching and all other ways they can, they will persuade the people from it."*

In fact, this attempt to induce the clergy to take the Oath of Supremacy proved such a complete failure that in December the Queen sent orders to the visitors to stop all further proceeding. The extent of the failure may be gathered from the fact that out of 9400 beneficed clergy they could only return the names of 806 as having subscribed the oath. Their report may be seen amongst the Domestic State Papers. Most of the clergy refused even to present themselves before the visitors.

Mr. Simpson, in his Life of Blessed Campion (pp. 139-140), gives the following summary of the evidence of State Papers: "In the visitation of the province of York in August and September, 1559, out of 90 clergymen summoned, 21 came and took the oath, 36 came and refused to swear, 7 were absent without proctors, 16 were absent with proctors. Yet of the 36 the lists of Bridgewater and Sanders only contain 5 names; of the 7, 4; of the 16, 7. If those lists are perfect, it proves that the rest were connived at and perhaps retained their livings till their death."

In a note the following further information is given as regards the province of York:—

"S.P.O. Dom. Eliz. vol. x. The calculations and the lists are based on the detailed proceedings in which all the names are given. At the end of the volume there

---

* Dodd, vol. II. Appendix xxxiii.

is an abstract of the numbers of rectors, vicars, and curates who refused to attend the visitation when summoned. The numbers are 158 for York diocese, 85 for Chester, 36 for Durham, and 35 for Carlisle; total 314. There is no abstract of the numbers who attended and refused the oath. Probably the visitation was never completed, but broken off by the Queen's letters. The book, however, proves that in York province certainly 370 clergymen—probably 600—either refused to swear or would have refused if they had been pressed. This gives a total much higher than 172, which Protestant historians give as the number of recusant clergymen for the whole of England, or than 250, the number stated by Allen and Bridgewater after Sanders" (p. 374).

As regards the province of Canterbury, he says, "In the province of Canterbury we hear of the dean and canons of Winchester Cathedral, the warden and fellows of the college, and the master of Holy Cross, all refusing the oath (S.P.O. Dom. June 30, 1559). Yet only four of them are in Bridgewater's list." And for the whole country, "The visitors returned for the whole province the total of 49 recusants and 786 conformists (Lansdowne Ms. cix. p. 7), significantly omitting the absentees. Thus, out of the 8911 parishes (S.P.O. Dom. Eliz. vol. cvi. no. 7) and 9400 beneficed clergymen (Camden, Eliz. i. 32) we find only 806 subscribers, while all the bishops and 85 others expressly refused to subscribe, and the rest were absentees. The assertion, then, of Camden, that only 189 clergymen were deprived in this visitation, proves nothing. Archbishop Parker had orders 'not to push anyone to extremities on account of his oath.' But Sanders and Bridgewater give many more names."

The Government were not prepared to deal with such wholesale recusancy. They were far too wise to attempt to do so, and the result was that three years' grace were given in many cases; while only a few, and those the heads of the clergy, were deprived in this visitation, *i.e.*, by the end of 1559, as a warning to others.

Camden puts the number down as 189, and Collier 243 but this included, as a rule, the bishops, deans, archdeacons, prebendaries and heads of colleges,—in fact, the pick of the clergy. Out of this grain of fact Church Defenders have built up a mountain of fable. Some have even gone so far as to say that all the old clergy of the Church of England conformed to the new order of things with this exception. But this estimate includes only those *deprived* of their livings in the visitation of 1559, which, beginning in May and ending in December, lasted only six months. No attempt has been made to estimate the total number of clergy (1) who resigned rather than face persecution, (2) who refused to take the oath and were not deprived in the visitation of 1559, (3) who were deprived in subsequent visitations, (4) who were ejected to make room for the married clergy removed in Mary's reign. That the number was very great we have abundant evidence.

    1. As to those who resigned, Cox, writing to Peter Martyr after the visitation of 1559 was over, says: "The popish priests among us are daily relinquishing their ministry lest, as they say, they should be compelled to give their sanction to heresies."* Lever writes to Bullingham, July 10, 1560, six months after, stating the result to be: "Many of our parishes have no clergyman, and some dioceses are without a bishop. And out of that very small number who administer the sacraments throughout this great country, there is scarcely one in a hundred, who is both able and willing to preach the word of God."† And Collier says: "Upon the Catholic clergy throwing up their preferments the necessities of the Church required the admitting of some mechanics into orders."‡

    2. We have seen that in this first visitation only 806 clergy were prevailed upon to take the Oath of Supremacy, and that the attempt to induce the rest of the clergy to do

---

* Zurich Letters, xxviii.
† Ibid. xxxv.   ‡ Bk. vi. 465.

so had to be given up as hopeless. Cox writes on May 21, 1559, thus of the attitude of the clergy: "At length many of the nobility and vast numbers of the common people began by degrees to come to their senses, but of the clergy none at all, for the whole body remained unmoved."*

3. The long and numerous lists given in Rymer† of presentations by the Queen to prebends, rectories and vicarages vacant by the *deprivation* of the last incumbent tell their own tale of the action of the Government subsequent to the visitation of 1559 now in one place, now in another. In 1561, a second general visitation began. In many dioceses a third of the parishes were vacant. In the Archdeaconry of Norwich 80 parishes were without clergy. In the Archdeaconry of Norfolk 180, and in that of Suffolk 130, were in the same condition.‡ In most of them the voice of the priest was silent in the desolate aisles. The children grew up unbaptised, and the dead buried their dead. So awful was the spiritual desolation of the country that "carpenters, blacksmiths and uneducated men of every mechanic art" had to be ordained to read the service. Nothing short of the direst necessity could have forced the government to resort to the extreme measure of filling the old parsonages with such a set of clowns who were sure to bring disgrace upon their cloth. They were too ignorant to preach and had to be provided with the book of Homilies. They were also so gross in their manners that the Queen had to interfere to check their nuptial vagaries. Cecil charged the Bishop of Lichfield with making seventy clergymen in one day for moneyed consideration. "Some were tailors, some stonemasons, and others craftsmen." "I am sure," he said, "the greatest part of them are not able to keep decent houses."§

* Zurich Letters, xi.   † xv. 542, &c., &c.
‡ Strype's Annals, vol. i. See Froude, vii. p. 16,
§ MS. Domestic, Feb 27th, 1585. Notes on a conversation between the Queen and Cecil.

This is no fancy picture. In the *Calendar of State Papers, Domestic, 1601–1603 with addenda 1547–1565* (p. 576) will be found a return made by the new Protestant bishops of the livings vacant in their various dioceses in 1565, frequently with the name of the last incumbent. Eleven of them make no return but of the rest, the following is the state of Durham diocese, which there is no reason to suppose formed any exception to the general condition of the country:—" Durham 3; with note that in many parishes, especially in Northumberland, the vicars have to serve from two to five chapels each— far from the parish churches which have no priests unless it be vagabond Scots who dare not abide in their country;—that they were better served when they belonged to abbeys; that in Durham were great parishes from which the Queen receives large revenues, and yet they have neither parson or vicar but a lewd priest to whom the Queen allows £4 or £5 a year, and some have no curate at all."

If, then, all the clergy but 189 had conformed in 1559, what had become of them in so short a time? And whence the necessity for the searching visitation of 1561 and the savage statute of 1562, which visited recusancy with the penalties of *præmunire* and high treason? Hallam, adverting to this admission of illiterate mechanics to the ministry, remarks: "This seems to show that more churches were empty by the desertion of popish incumbents than the foregoing note would lead us to suppose. I believe that many went off to foreign parts who had complied in 1559, and others were put out of their livings. The Roman Catholics make out a larger list than Burnet's calculation (200) allows. It appears from an account sent in to the privy council by Parkhurst, bishop of Norwich, in 1562, that in his diocese more than a third of the benefices were vacant (Strype's Annals, vol. 1). But in Ely, out of 152 cures, only 52 were served in 1560" (L. of Parker, 72).*

* Hallam, p. 183.

4. Of the numbers removed to make room for the return of the married clergy, ejected in Mary's reign, as well as of those who resigned when more pressure was brought to bear to force them to take the oaths, Hallam says: "It is moreover highly probable that others resigned their preferments afterwards when the casuistry of their Church grew more scrupulous. It may be added that the visitors restored the married clergy who had been dispossessed in the preceding reign; which would of course considerably augment the number of sufferers for Popery."* Burnet (vol. iii. 226) gives the number of these married clergy ejected in Mary's reign as 3000, Lingard estimates them at 1500.† It is clear from Collier's list that the lesser clergy ejected to make room for these men is not included in his estimate of those deprived in the visitation of 1559.

In the case of those clergy who were weak enough to temporize, the reforming party was quite alive to the fact that their outward conformity was only from motives of policy and implied no change of belief. Camden observes, "It seemed good to many of the popish priests both for their own sakes and the cause of religion to swear obedience to the sovereign, rejecting the authority of the Pope with this very purpose of excluding Protestants‡ from their churches and of helping those who had resigned. They look upon this as pious prudence and somewhat meritorious and hoped that the Roman Pontiff would by his authority dispense them from their oath."§

It is true that many Catholics attended the Church services till their doing so came to be looked upon as a distinctive sign of their having renounced their religion,

---

* Const. Hist. p. iii.   † Hallam, p. 104.
§ Writers of this school always speak of the new teachers as Protestants. They were evidently not aware of the theory of religious *identity* between themselves and the old Church. *Diversity* was their plea.
‡ See also Collier, Bk. vi. p. 436.

on the same grounds on which till recently they went to the Protestant minister to obtain the civil recognition of their marriages, simply to avoid the legal penalties of not doing so. They persuaded themselves that the private observance of their own religion elsewhere would excuse a formal obedience to the civil power. "There is nothing in this statement of fact which serves to countenance the very unfair misrepresentation lately given, as if the Roman Catholics generally had acquiesced in the Anglican worship believing it to be substantially the same as their own. They frequented our churches because the law compelled them so to do, not out of a notion that very little change had been made by the Reformation."*

Hence it is clear how baseless are those *imaginative reconstructions* of English History, whose object is to persuade the unlearned public that the religious movement of Queen Elizabeth's reign was the Church of England's own doing. On the contrary, nothing can be more certain than the fact that as a body the whole *spiritualty* of England protested earnestly against it. For (1) the whole bench of bishops except Kitchin of Llandaff preferred to suffer deprivation and imprisonment rather than soil their hands with it. (2) Of the rest of the governing body of the Church, according to Collier, 12 deans, 14 archdeacons, 60 canons, 15 heads of colleges at Oxford and Cambridge, 20 doctors, and 100 of the well preferred clergy shared the fate of the 14 bishops. (3) Of the lesser clergy besides those deprived in the visitation of 1559, spoken of by Camden and others, a large number, according to Burnet some 3,000, were expelled to make room for the married clergy removed in the previous reign. Others resigned, some before, some after this visitation. Others were deprived, now here, now there. Still, so stout was their resistance that, when the three years' grace allowed in many cases had elapsed,

* Hallam, p. 121, note.

a fresh visitation, that of 1561, became necessary in order to break down their opposition. And as this, too, was ineffectual, the statute of 1562 which visited recusancy with the penalty of death, was passed, a fact in itself sufficient to explode the absurd fable that with the exception of between one and two hundred, the English clergy freely consented to take the Oath of Supremacy and to conform to the new gospel. Of course there were a certain number, who were "men of both gospels," ready to conform to any change, but their conduct is a proof of nothing but their own want of principle. Their action counts for very little when opposed to that of the lawful rulers of the Church of England, *viz.*, to that of the bishops and as a body the whole spiritualty of the land.

The Faith of the Ancient English Church concerning the Holy Eucharist.

By THE VERY REV.
J. S. PROVOST NORTHCOTE.

We are indebted for the following tract to the Rev. T. E. BRIDGETT, C.SS.R., who has kindly allowed us to compile it from his *History of the Holy Eucharist in Great Britain.* It is taken almost entirely from chapters VIII. and IX. of the first volume of that excellent work. A few additions have been made from Lingard's *Anglo-Saxon Church.*

IT is the teaching of the Catholic Church that when the words of consecration are pronounced by the priest in Holy Mass, the substance of the bread and wine are changed into the substance of the Body and Blood of Christ.

To those who deny Creation, such a doctrine as this has of course no meaning; but in itself, and to those who reflect on what they believe, it is surely much harder to say, "I believe that God called into being things that were not," than to say "I believe that God, after becoming man, has instituted, for most wise and loving reasons, the change of our bodies' food into His own substantial Presence Who is the Bread of Life." His Divine Power changed man from senseless clay into a living being of flesh and blood, yet imposed on him at the same time the law that he should support that flesh and blood on the fruits of the earth whence Adam was taken. Is it then not conceivable that, having redeemed that fallen creature, He should find the means in harmony with His double nature to make him feed on his true life? Thus the outward forms of bread and wine remind him of the dust from which he was taken, while the hidden Presence reminds him of the end for which he was created, and of the redemption by which that end is again placed within his reach.

Neither will it be denied, by those who believe the Holy Scriptures, that the doctrine of Transubstantiation is in perfect harmony with the history of God's prodigies both in the Old and New Testaments. He converted a dry rod into a living serpent, and a living serpent He changed back again into a dry rod; is it then incredible that bread and wine should be transformed into the living life-giving Flesh and Blood of Christ, and that, when the outward species are corrupted, the Flesh and Blood should cease to be present, and the former substances, as some think, be again restored?* The Son of God Himself took flesh at the word of a woman by the operation of the Holy Ghost; is it incredible to Christians that by the power of the same Holy Ghost, at the consecration of the priest using Christ's words and doing so by His own command, He should be again as it were incarnate? He changed water into wine to grace an earthly nuptial feast; is it contrary to analogy that He should change wine into His Blood in celebrating the perpetual banquet with the souls of men? During the days of His mortality he showed His Body at one time walking on the waves of the sea, at another lifted up from the earth and all glorious at His Transfiguration. Is it to be thought so strange that, now It is glorified above the heavens, He should for our sakes reduce It to conditions which exceed our experience and baffle our comprehension? He appeared and disappeared suddenly and mysteriously during the forty days He spent on earth after His resurrection, passing through the closed sepulchre and penetrating the closed doors; was it not to accustom us to modes of being remote from ordinary laws? And lastly, He multiplied visibly yet incomprehensibly the loaves of bread, distributing them by His apostles' hands till,

* It must not be supposed however that this is an article of faith: various opinions on this matter have been held in Catholic schools of theology.

after feeding thousands, the fragments that remained far surpassed in bulk the loaves unbroken; shall we then murmur when He promises to feed the millions of His Church on His Flesh which is meat indeed, and His Blood which is drink indeed, and shall we say: "This saying is hard, who can bear it?" "How can this man give us His Flesh to eat?"

It is true, indeed, that in the incidents just mentioned the bodily senses of the spectators bore testimony to the reality of the change; but the words of our Blessed Lord to St. Thomas suffice to teach us that the evidence of the senses is not the most perfect foundation on which faith can be based. Transubstantiation is a miracle in which our senses can be of no use to us, for it takes place in a region into which the senses cannot penetrate—in the region not of appearances but of substances, which are impervious to the senses as our own souls are: nevertheless our Blessed Lord, in preparing us for belief in this invisible miracle, vouchsafed to appeal to the sight and other senses. He wrought two miracles in particular—that of Cana in Galilee, and the multiplication of the loaves and fishes—of the truth and reality of which the senses *could* judge, in order that we might be prepared and disposed to believe His word with respect to corresponding miracles in the Blessed Sacrament of which, from the very necessity of the case, the senses were precluded from judging.

That the miracle of the loaves and fishes was intended, amongst other ends, for the very purpose of confirming our faith in the corresponding Eucharistic miracle is clear from this, that our Lord made it the occasion of announcing to his disciples the future gift of His own Body and Blood as the food of life. When the Jews on the following day had found Him in the synagogue of Capharnaum, He reproached them for labouring too earnestly for the meat which perisheth, and bade them think more of that which endureth unto life everlasting, "which," He said, "the Son of man *will* give you." The word was not lost upon His hearers. It set them thinking and speaking of the manna with which their fathers had been fed in the wilderness. Jesus told them in reply that His Father would give them true bread from heaven that would give life to the world; and added that He was Himself that bread of life and that He had come down from heaven. The Jews, thinking that they knew all about His life and parentage, asked how He could have come down from heaven. Without vouchsafing a direct answer to this question, Jesus repeated His assertion and made a further step in the unfolding of His doctrine by saying, "The bread that I will give is My Flesh for the life of the world." The Jews therefore strove among themselves saying: "How can this man give us His Flesh to eat?" Again our Blessed Lord gives no explanation of their difficulty, but insists again and again with every variety of form, on the necessity and blessedness of eating the Flesh of the Son of man and drinking His Blood. After this many of His disciples went back and walked no more with Him. Then Jesus said to the twelve, "Will you also go away?" And Simon Peter answered Him, "Lord, to whom shall we go? Thou hast the words of eternal life. And we have believed and have known that Thou art the Christ, the Son of God." That is to say, he did not understand how our Lord's words were to be fulfilled any more than the Jews did, but he accepted his Master's words with unhesitating faith. And when on the eve of His Passion the apostles saw our Lord again take bread in His Sacred Hands and repeat the same action which had accompanied His miracle on the mount,—when they saw Him now, as then, look up to heaven, and bless and break, and when His words, His creative and transforming words, at last fell on their ear—"Take eat, this is My Body, this is My Blood"—then in a moment they comprehended that scheme of loving preparation and the full meaning of that mysterious discourse at Capharnaum. Thenceforward both the apostles themselves and all priests and bishops succeeding them, repeating the divine action in obedience to our Lord's command, could with the most certain faith repeat the words of St. Paul, "The chalice of benediction which we bless, is it not the communion of the Blood of Christ? And the bread which we break is it not the partaking of the Body of the Lord?" (1. Cor. x. 16.)

Let thus much be said on the doctrine of the Holy Eucharist before we enter upon the immediate subject of the following pages, which is, not to establish the truth of the doctrine of Transubstantiation, but to show that the same doctrine was held on this subject in the ancient Church of England as is held by Catholics to-day. All are agreed that this was the doctrine of the Church of England for some centuries before the reformation, but it is pretended that it was first introduced into this country by the Italo-Norman primates, Lanfranc and St. Anselm, when it supplanted the more ancient and pure Protestant or quasi-Protestant doctrine which had before prevailed.

To all Catholics who know that the Church can never err, because she is the Spouse of Christ and has received the Holy Ghost for her dowry, there is no need to prove that the Church has always and everywhere been one in faith regarding the Blessed Sacrament of the Altar; but the change we have indicated is so persistently asserted by many writers that it is worth while to expose the falsehood of their statements.

"This island at present," wrote Venerable Bede in the eight century, "in the languages of five nations, examines and confesses one and the same science of the sublimest truth and true sublimity, viz., in those of the Angles, Britons, Scots, and Picts, and Latins; and this last, by the study of the Scriptures, has become common to all the rest." This testimony to the absolute unity in faith of the different Churches throughout Great Britain is confirmed by every document which has come down to us from whatever source. That there were disputes between the ancient British Church and the Roman missionaries who came with St. Augustine is of course notorious; but these very disputes bring out, in the most incontrovertible and convincing way, how absolute was the unanimity between them as to all articles of faith. There were antagonisms, jealousies and disputes on points of discipline ; and in zeal of controversy, every difference, even in the shape of a tonsure, was magnified and sometimes made a big word of reproach ; yet not once did there escape from the lips of either party a reproach implying defect in faith, or error in worship. Discrepancies had arisen in the celebration of the Easter festival, from different reckoning of time, not from diversity of principle. As to the mystery which was commemorated at Easter, or the rite of commemoration, there was no discrepancy. St. Bede does indeed affirm that, besides their error in computing the time of Easter, the Britons "did also very many other things contrary to ecclesiastical unity." It is however certain that, whatever was the nature of these things, they in no way affected faith, morals or worship, for St. Augustine was content to tolerate the diversity, provided only they would reform the Easter cycle and complete the ceremonies of Baptism. It is not certain in what this defect consisted: as regards the nature of British peculiarities in other matters, we are left to conjecture. They cannot have been of great importance, since almost the only one that became a topic of contention was the shape of the ecclesiastical and monastic tonsure. It is inconceivable then that there can have been any difference between the contending parties on so vital a doctrine of the Christian faith as the Real Presence in the Sacrament of the Altar, the nature of the Holy Sacrifice of the Mass, or the intentions for which it should be offered. As to such matters no breath of accusation was ever heard on either side. Nevertheless, Protestant writers are found who dare to contrast "the advance of corruption in government, in faith, in doctrine, which was being made under Papal leadership throughout the rest of Europe, with the steadfast adherence to primitive truth and discipline which distinguished the isolated British Church ;" and they point to the conference of St. Augustine with the British bishops in 603 as one of the tide marks of time, as the meeting of the Christianity of the year 400 with that of 600 ; and at a still later period in the history of our country, writers of the same class speak of an "unyielding array of testimony which echoes from the whole theological school of ancient England against the new divinity of Lanfranc" in the doctrine of Transubstantiation.

It is the object of the following pages to show how unfounded are these charges of corruption, of change or of disagreement. The information that has come down to us regarding the faith of the ancient Britons, is in many points scanty and obscure, but we have seen that in all important matters it agreed with that of the later Anglo-Saxon Church. We shall proceed then, to set before our readers some testimony as to the faith of the Anglo-Saxons with regard to the Blessed Sacrament of the Altar.

A modern Catholic reading the life of St. Columba, written by Adamnan in 696, or the Ecclesiastical History of England, written by Bede in 736, will find every formula familiar to himself and expressing his faith exactly, as well as adequately. Protestants, on the contrary, whether Calvinists, Zwinglians, Lutherans, or High Church Anglicans, are uneasy at such language, carefully avoid it themselves, and sometimes even distort or evade it when making quotations. To give an example. Bede relates that King Ethelbert gave St. Augustine the old Church of St. Martin, and that "in this they began to meet, to chant psalms, to offer prayers, to celebrate Masses (*missas facere*), to preach, to baptize." In translating this, Carte says they preached and performed "other acts of devotion ;" Collier, that they "preached, baptized and performed all the solemn offices of religion ; " Churton, that they "administered the sacraments."

Such vague expressions show well enough a want of sympathy with Bede even as regards so simple and venerable an expression as Mass. How much less then would Protestants use or understand the various periphrases so familiar to Bede and to all our early writers as "the celebration of the most sacred mysteries, the heavenly and mysterious Sacrifice, the offering of the Victim of Salvation, the Sacrifice of the Mediator, the Sacrifice of the Body and Blood of Christ, the memorial of Christ's great Passion, the renewal of the Passion and death of the Lamb!" All these expressions are used by Bede in his History and Homilies; and for the Blessed Sacrament Itself, as distinct from the rite of offering it to God—besides the more common designations *Hostia* and *Sacrificium* (in the vernacular, Housel),—they would speak of the Saving Victim of the Lord's Body and Blood, the Victim without an equal, a particle of the Sacrifice of the Lord's offering. These expressions are also found in Bede. We quote two passages from him. "As often as the solemnity of the Mass is celebrated, that most sacred Body and that precious Blood of the Lamb with which we have been redeemed from sin are immolated anew to God for the benefit of our salvation." And again, "Christ washes us from our sins in His Blood daily, when the memory of His Blessed Passion is renewed on the altar; when the creatures of bread and wine are made to pass by means of the inexplicable hallowing of the Spirit into the Sacrament of Christ's Body and Blood; which Body is no longer slain, which Blood is no longer shed, by the hands of infidels to their ruin, but received by the mouths of the faithful to their salvation."

Adamnan the Scot speaks of the Sacrifice of Mass, the Sacrificial mystery, the mysteries of the most Holy Sacrifice; and he tells us of the priest at the altar who performs the mysteries of Christ, consecrates the mysteries of the Eucharist, celebrates the solemnities of Masses. If we turn to the writings of Eddi, of St. Boniface, or St. Egbert, or to the decrees of early councils we find the same or similar phrases varied in every possible way to express the mystery, the sublimity of which was beyond human utterance. A multitude of verbs were in common use to designate the action of the priest at the altar. "*Missam cantare* or *canere*" might designate the whole action, though with special allusion to the vocal prayers. "*Missam facere*," "*offerre*," "*celebrare*," "*agere*," would also refer to the whole divine action ; "*conficere,*" "*immolare,*" "*libare,*" regarded the *Hostia* or Victim which was our Lord's Body and Blood or our Divine Lord Himself; and the secret operation by which the bread and wine were changed into our Lord's Body and Blood was indicated by every word by which Transubstantiation can be expressed, among which we find "*transferre,*" "*commutare,*" "*transcribere,*" "*transformare,*" "*convertere.*" In spite of all this evidence, which exists in abundance, and lies, so to say, on the very surface of Anglo-Saxon religious literature, there are still Protestants who affirm that Transubstantiation was unknown to the Anglo-Saxon Church. Perhaps it will be useless to offer further proofs to those whose minds are prejudiced, yet it may be of service to some to remind them that with equal plausibility it might be denied that Catholics hold the doctrine of Transubstantiation at the present day. How, it may be asked, do Catholics now succeed in expressing their belief not only to themselves but even to their opponents? Whatever answer is given to this question, it is easy to show that the very same tests, when applied to the Anglo-Saxon Church, will give the same result. It might be said for example that modern Catholics hold the Real Presence of our Lord not in some vague and undefined mode as many Anglicans do, but that they make formal and explicit declaration of their belief in a change of substance ; or that they not only call the Sacrament our Lord's Flesh and Blood, but speak of it as containing Christ Himself; or again that reports are current among them of miracles and visions attesting the Real Presence of Him Who died on the Cross. Let us then take these three tests and see how they apply to the faith of the disciples of St. Augustine, St. Paulinus, or St. Aidan.

I. First, then, Catholics are very explicit in saying what they mean by speaking of the Body and Blood of Christ. They use expressions that do not admit of being taken vaguely and metaphorically. They necessarily imply change of substance. Can anything in their way go beyond the following words of Aimo, writing in

A.D. 841: "It would be the most monstrous madness to doubt that the substance of the bread and wine which are placed upon the altar, is made the Body and Blood of Christ by the mysterious action of the priest and thanksgiving, God effecting this by His divine grace and secret power. We believe then, and faithfully confess and hold, that the substance of bread and wine, by the operation of divine power, the nature, I say, of bread and wine is substantially converted into another substance, that is, into Flesh and Blood. Surely it is not impossible to the omnipotence of Divine wisdom to change nature once created, into whatever It may choose, since when It pleased It created them from nothing. He who could make something out of nothing, can find no difficulty in changing one thing to another. It is thus the invisible Priest who converts visible creatures into the substance of His own Flesh and Blood by His secret power. In this which we call the Body and Blood of Christ, the taste and appearance of bread and wine remain to remove all horror from those who receive, but the nature of the substance is altogether changed into the Body and Blood of Christ. The senses tell us one thing, faith tells us another. The senses can only tell what they perceive, but the intelligence tells us of the true Flesh and Blood of Christ, and faith confesses it again."

Could anyone mistake the meaning of the following letter addressed to a Catholic priest: "I beg you will not forget your friend's name in your holy prayer. Store it up in one of the caskets of your memory and bring it out in fitting time, when you have consecrated bread and wine into the substance of the Body and Blood of Christ." Are not these words explicit? Well, they were used in writing to a Catholic priest; but it was more than a thousand years ago,—he who used them was Alcuin, the disciple of Bede, the master of Aimo.

II. We proceed now to our second test. Modern Catholics speak of the Holy Eucharist as containing Christ Himself. This follows necessarily from our belief in the presence of His Flesh and Blood, for these can now neither be really separated one from the other, nor from our Lord's Soul, much less from His Divinity. Yet at the present day there are Anglican writers who admit with us that Christ's Flesh and Blood are present beneath the veils of bread and wine, yet deny that He Himself is there to receive our adoration. They seem to have meditated little on our Lord's words: "He that eateth My Flesh and drinketh My Blood *abideth in Me and I in him.* As the Living Father hath sent Me and I live by the Father, so he that *eateth* Me the same also shall live by Me." But our forefathers pondered more deeply on divine things. The very earliest document of the faith of the Anglo-Saxon Church is the letter written by St. Gregory to St. Augustine. In this he contrasts the angel who appeared on Sinai with the Lord of the angels Who is contained in the Blessed Sacrament. "If so much purity," he says, "was then required, when God spoke to the people by the means of a subject creature, how much ought those to be purer who receive the *Body of Almighty God*, lest they be burdened with the greatness of that unutterable mystery." The same great Doctor of the Church and of the English in particular says in his Book of Dialogues—and this volume was translated into Anglo-Saxon by Werfirth of Worcester, one of the literary assistants of King Alfred—"This sacrifice of His Body and Blood saveth the soul from everlasting destruction; for it reneweth to us through the mystery the death of the only begotten Son of God, who truly arose from the dead and after that dieth no more nor hath death any more dominion over Him; yet though He be living in Himself immortal and incorruptible *He is again sacrificed for us* in the mystery of the holy oblation." The following prayer for the blessing of the altar canopy or the Ciborium, gives another clear proof of the faith of the Anglo-Saxon Church; "Almighty and everlasting God, we beseech Thy ineffable clemency that Thou wouldst deign to pour Thy heavenly blessing upon this covering of Thy venerable altar, upon which Thy only-begotten Son, our Lord Jesus Christ, Who is the propitiation for our sins, is constantly immolated by the hands of the faithful." In the consecration of an altar the Anglo-Saxon bishop prayed for the blessing of God that "on that altar His secret power may turn the elements chosen for the Sacrifice into the Body and Blood of the Redeemer, and by an invisible change, transform them into the holy Sacrifice of the Lamb; to the end that as the Word was made Flesh, so the nature of the oblation being blest, may be improved into the substance of the Word, and that which before was food, may here be made eternal life." Is it not clear that the Church which made use of this prayer, containing such an accumulation of phrases, all evidently intended to express one and the same doctrine, taught that the Eucharistic elements lying on the altar were there substantially changed by an invisible power into the Body and Blood of Christ?

III. The third test which we proposed of Anglo-Saxon faith was this. There are many stories current amongst modern Catholics regarding visions, apparitions, and miracles, by which the Real Presence of Jesus Christ beneath the sacramental veil has been attested. Protestants may consider these to be either delusions or impostures, but they accept them as evidence of our belief. Why, then, if similar stories were current among the Anglo-Saxons, should not the same conclusion be drawn? Now there were many such, and two shall be here related in the very words of those who first recorded them. The first is the vision of St. Edward. It is thus related by the Abbot St. Ælred who was born about forty years after St. Edward's death.

"In the monastery of St. Peter, which he had rebuilt or enlarged, before the altar of the Blessed Trinity, the most Christian king was assisting at the mysteries of our redemption. Count Leofric, whose memory is in benediction and who can never be named without reverence and spiritual joy, was present, together with his wife Godgiva. The holy count was standing at a little distance from the king. The Holy Mystery was being celebrated at the altar, and the Divine Sacraments were in the priest's hands, when behold, He Who is beauteous beyond the sons of men, Christ Jesus, appeared standing on the altar visible to the bodily eyes of both, and with His right hand stretched over the king He blessed him with the sign of the Cross. The king bowing his head adored the Presence of Divine Majesty, and with humble posture paid honour to so great a blessing. But the Count not knowing what was passing in the mind of the king, and wishing him to share in so great a vision, began to draw near to him. But the king, knowing his thoughts, said: 'Stop, Leofric, stop; I see what you see.' They both give themselves up to prayers and tears, and are inebriated with the fulness of God's house and drink of the torrents of His delights. When Mass is over they converse on the heavenly vision. The king forbids the Count to mention it to any one during his life. In this he imitates our Lord after the transfiguration. The Count merely tells it to a religious at Worcester in confession, binding him also to secrecy, but begging him to write it that it may be revealed later on. This was done, and so it became known after the king's death."

Our second history shall be that of St. Odo, Archbishop of Canterbury, who died in 959. We have two versions of it, one in the life of the Saint by Eadmar, another written a whole century earlier (A.D. 959-1005) by a monk of Ramsey who had been intimate with St. Oswald, Odo's nephew, and had probably learnt from him what he relates. He writes as follows: "On a certain day when he (*i.e.*, Archbishop Odo) was offering pontifically to the great King (*i.e.*, to God) the worthy ministry of the Divine Sacrament, and was celebrating apart with his household the paschal feast of the glorious Lamb of God, that heavenly Lamb deigned to console him by the following miracle. After the recitation of the Gospel and the offering of the Divine Gift, and when his soul was full of compunction and his eyes flowing with tears, such as are often shed by the faithful and happy worshippers of God amidst these holy mysteries, this trusted friend of the Redeemer began with chaste hands to touch the species of His Body (*effigiem*). While he was doing this he beheld an ancient miracle renewed in our times: for a drop of Blood flowed from the true Flesh of Christ's body. On beholding this most clearly with his eyes he marvelled; his mind was filled with fear and he was troubled in spirit. He calls immediately a faithful attendant who was near at hand and secretly shows him the miracle. To whom the priest replied; ' Rejoice, most reverend father, since Christ the Son of God has to-day so honoured thee that thou hast been worthy to see with thy bodily eyes Him Who is over all, God blessed for ever. Pray I beseech you the power of the ineffable God to make His Body return to its first form.' And when he had prayed, he arose, and found It as It was before, and received It with exultation of soul. On that day he ordered all the poor, the pilgrims, the orphans and widows, to be assembled, to whom, in honour of so great a miracle he commanded that a solemn feast should be given. Thus it came to pass that, while the head of the Kentish city was feeding on a heavenly banquet, the members were feasted on earthly food."

The fact of the great banquet given to the poor by St. Odo in honour of some great prodigy at the altar can scarcely be called in question, related as it is both by Eadmar and by this contemporary writer. That the prodigy consisted in the truth of Transubstantiation being made visible is also related by both; and let him deny or explain away the miracle who will; at least this is evident that the Saxon writer of the tenth century held exactly the same faith in this regard as the Norman writer of the eleventh century. Moreover, this monk of Ramsey testifies not only to the faith, but to the antiquity of the faith, of the Anglo-Saxon Church in Transubstantiation. He says that St. Odo beheld an *ancient miracle* renewed in our times; in fact similar histories are related from the earliest periods both in East and West; by St. Gregory of Tours in the sixth century, by St. Arsenius in the fifth, by Palladius in the fourth, by St. Cyprian in the third. Or to keep to this country, John the deacon expressly declares that in his time (about 875) a history was wont to be read in the English Church about the miracles of St. Gregory the Great—how that at his prayers on one occasion the Sacred Host took the form of a finger dropping with blood to convict the incredulity of a lady ; so also has Paschasius Radbert, writing in the middle of the ninth century, told us a very similar vision granted at the prayer of a priest named Plagils in the church of St. Ninian at Whithorne in Galloway, and he says that this was read in the Acts of the English.

We take our leave of this part of the subject by quoting the words of Lanfranc : "No one even slightly versed in ecclesiastical history and the lives of the holy Fathers is ignorant of these miracles, and although the writings in which they are recorded have not that superior authority which belongs to those of the prophets and apostles, yet at least they prove this—that all the faithful before us from the earliest times had the same faith as we have."

We have now laid before our readers a mass of evidence, to which much more might have been adduced, abundantly sufficient to show what was the faith of the Anglo-Saxon Church with reference to the Blessed Sacrament. It remains to enquire what can be added on the other side; and the answer must be given that there is one solitary witness: and even he, when he comes to be cross-examined, and his evidence closely sifted, is found to give but feeble support to the cause of which he is the main, if not the only stay.

Who, then, is the witness? Ælfric, a monk of Cerne in Dorsetshire, and in due time an Abbot, about the beginning of the eleventh century, but, as Dr. Lingard has shown neither Archbishop of Canterbury, nor of York, nor Bishop of Crediton, though some of his biographers have claimed these dignities for him. He was a diligent and not inelegant compiler and translator of religious works, and amongst these he compiled two sets of Homilies, each a sufficient course for one year. In these he uniformly follows the typical method of

Scriptural interpretation. There is not any action, or event, or name mentioned in the Sacred Text which does not in his opinion teem with mystery. It may have a literal but it has also a "ghostly" signification; it expresses one thing but it also "betokeneth" another.

Before we proceed to examine what he has written, let it be clearly stated that the question of his faith or orthodoxy has nothing to do with that of the Anglo-Saxon Church, since neither by position nor reputation was he her representative. If Ælfric were shown to be Protestant in his doctrine, his doctrine was singular and his opinions erroneous. There is no man better entitled to speak on this subject than Dr. Lingard, who gave to Anglo-Saxon literature and institutions a lifelong attention. His judgment is as follows: "If Ælfric indeed taught Protestant doctrine, he must have been the first who taught it, for it was not the doctrine of those who wrote before him. Of it or of anything like to it not a trace is to be found in any document connected with the ancient British Church; not in the acts of her councils, not in the liturgical and euchological forms of her worship, not in the correspondence or biography or works of her writers, and I make this assertion with the greater confidence, not only because I have made the enquiry myself but also because it is now almost three hundred years since Archbishop Parker and his followers were challenged to produce the testimony of any other native writer in support of this supposed doctrine of Ælfric; and yet as far as I can learn no man to the present day has responded to the call. Undoubtedly they would have done so had it been in their power." He goes on to show how Mr. Soames in his *History of the Anglo-Saxon Church* has named Bede, Alcuin, and Erigena, but without venturing to quote them. Now we have already heard the clear testimony of Bede and Alcuin on the Catholic side, and Erigena was no Englishman, nor is it even certain that he ever set foot in this country. In 1879 appeared a new History of the Church of England. The author (Dr. Boultbee) as usual maintains that the

Saxon Church did not hold Transubstantiation, yet still the only authority quoted is Ælfric, and after alluding to other "leading church teachers" whom he does not name he concludes, "whatsoever else may be obscure in Ælfric's homily it is clear that he repudiates Transubstantiation." Now let us see what Ælfric has really said. I have perused very carefully the translation of his writings made by Mr. Thorpe, and I confess freely that there are in them many phrases of evil sound. Our readers shall judge for themselves.

Dr. Lingard gives the following extract from his homily on Easter Sunday as a fair sample of his doctrine. Having quoted the words of our Blessed Lord at the institution of the Sacrament and His declaration to the Jews in the sixth Chapter of St. John he proceeds thus: "Now some men have often enquired and do yet frequently make inquiries how the bread that is prepared out of corn and is baked through the heat of the fire, may be changed to Christ's Body and the wine that is wrung out of many berries be changed through any blessing to the Lord's Blood. Now say we to such men, that somethings are said of Christ by token, some in reality. Sooth then and real it is that Christ was born of a maiden and suffered death of His own will and was buried, and on this day rose from death. He is called bread through token, and a lamb, a lion and other things. . . . And yet He is not bread in his true kind nor a lamb, nor a lion. Why then is the Holy Housel called Christ's Body or His Blood if it be not truly that which it is called? Truly the bread and wine that are hallowed through the priest's Mass present one thing to man's senses outwardly and call up another thing to the minds of believers inwardly. Outwardly they are seen (or seem) bread and wine in appearance and taste; yet after the hallowing they are in sooth through ghostly mystery Christ's Body and His Blood.... Behold now we see two things in the water of baptism. It is in its own kind corruptible water; through ghostly mystery it hath a saving power. So also if we enquire into the Holy Housel according to its bodily appearance then we see that it is a corruptible and changeable creature; but if we are aware of the ghostly power that is in it, then we understand that life is therein which gives immortality to them who eat it with belief. Much difference is there between the invisible power of the Holy Housel and the visible appearance of its own kind. In kind it is corruptible bread and corruptible wine and according to the power of the Divine Word it is in sooth Christ's Body and His Blood; not however in bodily guise but after a ghostly manner. Truly the Body in which Christ suffered was born of the flesh of Mary with blood and bone, with a skin and sinews, with many limbs, and a reasonable soul giving life to it; and His ghostly body which we call the Housel is gathered of many corns, without blood and bone, limbless and soulless; and therefore we are to understand nothing therein after a bodily but everything is to be understood after a ghostly manner. Whatever is in the Housel that giveth to us the substance of life that is of the ghostly power and of invisible framing. Therefore the Holy Housel is called the mystery, because one thing is seen therein and another is understood... Many receive that Holy Body yet it is whole in every particle by ghostly mystery.., In sooth it is as we have already said Christ's Body and His Blood not after a bodily, but after a ghostly manner. Nor are you to enquire how it is made so, but to hold in your belief that it is made so."

Now we have admitted that there is something in this language unusual and ill sounding; nevertheless it is capable of being understood in a Catholic sense. Ælfric keeps insisting that the Body of Christ as received in the Eucharist is not the same Body that hung on the Cross; but these words may have a true sense or a false one. According to the Catholic faith It is essentially the same, yet not the same according to its mode of existence. Our Lord said of St. John the Baptist that he was Elias, John himself said that he was not. They spoke in different senses. The ancient Fathers who wrote against the Manichees insisted on free will as if to the neglect of grace; those who wrote against the Pelagians insisted on grace as it were to the disparagement of free will.

and the Holy Eucharist. 19

There was no real contradiction, but the opponents or objections required different language. So has it been with regard to the Eucharist. Against those who would adopt figurative interpretations of our Lord's words, Catholic writers will insist on the reality of His Flesh and Blood. Against men whose minds are gross and sensual, the same Catholic writers would insist on the presence being spiritual. In fact from the very nature of the question there will be the same double meaning and consequent ambiguity which is attached to the word "flesh" in Holy Scripture. St John speaks of the sons of God "who are born not of the flesh" and then immediately adds "and the Word was made Flesh." The eternal Son of God was made Flesh that the adopted sons of God might not be carnal. If we knew the state of mind of those for whom Ælfric was writing we could judge better about his meaning. He tells us at the beginning of the passage we have quoted that men were making enquiries about the mode of the Presence of Christ in the Holy Eucharist. If amongst these enquirers there were some who entertained gross views of what was meant by it, then the language of Ælfric is quite intelligible and Catholic. He is combating disbelief by proving that belief requires no such rude conceptions as they stumble at.

    I am confirmed in this view of Ælfric by the conduct and language of Lanfranc. How was it that the great champion of the doctrine of Transubstantiation against Berengarius never denounced the writings of Ælfric and never accused the Anglo-Saxon Church of heterodoxy with regard to the Eucharist? My answer is that Lanfranc saw in such teaching not an adverse theology but a different phrase of controversy. Lanfranc himself in his treatise against Berengarius written before he came to England uses the following words: "It may be truly said that we receive the very Body which was born of the Virgin yet not that very Body. It is that very Body if you consider its essence and the propriety and efficacy of its true nature. It is not the same, if you consider the appearance and the other qualities of bread and wine. This faith has been held from the beginning, and is still held by that Church which is called Catholic because it is spread throughout the world."

But we must go further and say that Ælfric's words are not merely capable of a Catholic interpretation: there are some of them that seem to admit of no other. He relates several miraculous apparitions of our Lord in the Blessed Sacrament; he concludes this very homily with one of them. "We read," he says, "in the *Vitæ Patrum* that two monks prayed to God for some manifestation respecting the Holy Eucharist, and after their prayer attended at Mass. There they saw a child lying on the altar at which the priest said Mass, and God's angel stood with a sword waiting till the priest broke the Housel, when the angel divided the child in twain upon the dish and poured the blood in the Chalice. But afterwards when they went to receive, it was changed again to bread and wine; and they received it thanking God for His manifestation."

Now if the story about St. Odo told by the monk of Ramsey and already quoted proves that the narrator held the doctrine of Transubstantiation, Ælfric's story must in fairness be held to prove the same. Why then are his ambiguous sentences about receiving the Body of Christ not in a bodily but a ghostly manner to be taken in a Protestant sense, as if he had never recorded this and similar miracles? And why on the contrary are not the miraculous apparitions which he does record to be taken as the key of his ambiguity, since it has been already said his language is capable of Catholic interpretation? When therefore he says "not bodily but spiritually," he does not mean what is implied by Protestants when they say " not really but figuratively," but he means as St. Augustine meant, and explained his meaning to be, " not in a gross sensible manner but in a hidden and mysterious manner." At the very least the illustration Ælfric has used clearly implies that in whatever way our Lord's Body is present, it is present objectively on the altar by virtue of consecration, and not subjectively in the recipient by virtue of faith.

To Dr. Boultbee's assertion, then, that whatsoever else may be obscure in Ælfric's homily on the Eucharist, it is clear that he repudiates Transubstantiation, I reply that, whatsoever else is obscure in his homily, at least his histories of the miraculous apparations are not obscure. And I invite Dr. Boultbee to use the same standard in judging of Ælfric as he does in writing of Paschasius Radbert when he says that "Paschasius unreservedly propounds the doctrine of Transubstantiation in the absolute sense, confirming it by stories of persons to whom had been vouchsafed the vision of the Sacred Body perceptible in the elements."

We have seen that although Ælfric is the only author who can be quoted with any plausibility in support of the Protestant view of the doctrine of the Anglo-Saxons, yet it is the custom to multiply him into a legion. Mr. Soames quotes Ælfric's words and none but his, yet he at once begins to speak of the "unyielding array of testimony against Lanfranc's new divinity which echoes from the whole theological school of ancient England." Dr. Boultbee says the same thing in other words. If I am asked how I explain the confident and reiterated assertions of these and similar writers, I reply that while some of them are the result of ignorance and prejudice, others may be accounted for without any impeachment of sincerity or learning.

In the first place it must be remembered that ever since Protestant controversy adopted a metaphorical interpretation of Scripture and of the Ancient Fathers regarding the Eucharist, Protestant ears have become habituated to the use of what to Catholics seem forced and unnatural metaphor. When a Protestant hears the communion called in a popular hymn,

> Rich banquet of His Flesh and Blood,

while he knows for certain that neither minister nor people believe in the Real Presence, he not only gets to use such language without any sense of incongruity, but when he meets with it in ancient Catholic writers he is easily persuaded that they meant no more than himself.

In the second place, just as it is a fundamental principle with Catholics that the Church's faith never varies, so it is a fundamental principle with Protestants that it is ever varying, that it never was steadfast and never will be. As with Catholics there is a presumption that an ancient writer who lived and died in the Church's communion intended at least to say what the Church now says, and every effort is made to interpret his words in a Catholic sense, so on the other hand, there is a presumption in the minds of many Protestants that an ancient writer could not have intended to say what Catholics now say. He may use the same language, but every ambiguity or omission is seized on as a reason for attributing to him another meaning.

In the third place, the mystery of the Eucharist is very profound. Those who have a perfectly correct faith, may easily err in theological statement, and the most correct theological statement may be easily misunderstood as erroneous by those whose minds are not trained in theological questions. Hence Catholic writers have been quoted as unorthodox, sometimes from their own difficulty in expressing their meaning, and still oftener from the inability of their readers to apprehend it. Thus Mr. Sharon Turner boldly says: "It is certain that the Transubstantiation of the Eucharist was not the established or universal belief of the Anglo-Saxons." Now what are the grounds of Mr. Turner's certainty? This alone, that in some Saxon Ecclesiastical Constitutions about the date of the Conquest, it is declared: "The Housel is Christ's Body, not bodily but spiritually; not the Body in which He suffered, but the Body about which He spoke when He blessed the loaf and wine." But Mr. Turner ought to have understood that although these words do not assert Transubstantiation, neither do they deny it. They would leave it *uncertain*, if we had no other grounds for judgment, whether their writer held it or not. Surely Catholics teach that our Lord's *and the Holy Eucharist.* 23

Body is spiritually present. And an eminent English theologian, a doctor of the Sorbonne, in the seventeenth century, in a work in which he aims at the most exact definitions of the Catholic faith, writes as follows: "The sense of our doctrine lies in this, that we profess the true and real body of Christ to be in this Sacrament, not in a bodily and passible, but in a spiritual way." And a yet more recent theologian, the late Cardinal Franzelin, insists upon it "that the mode of the Real Presence is altogether analogous to the mode of presence of spirits, nor can it be conceived or explained by us, except according to this analogy." We can only rise by certain steps towards our understanding of this Presence by considering what wonders are related of the bodies of saints, even in this life, what we are told of the "spiritual body" after the resurrection (1 Cor. xv. 44), and above all, what faith tells us of the state of our Lord's Body formerly on earth and now in heaven.

The above is one sense of the word spiritual as applied to the Blessed Sacrament, but it is not the only one. Sometimes it is opposed to gross or carnal; and very frequently among the Anglo-Saxons it means holy or consecrated as contrasted with what is profane or common.

A third and still more common use of the word by no means implies the absence of body, but its fitness or consecration for spiritual purposes. This may be seen clearly from one of the canons in Ælfric's collection, in which a church is called a "ghostly house," and "a prayer house hallowed to God for ghostly discourses." Here a ghostly discourse is not one without spoken words but one made up of words all tending to the edification of the soul; and the ghostly house is not a metaphorical house but one hallowed for God's worship. So too, when our Lord's Body is said to be ghostly, not natural, not mortal, not visible, not such as He suffered in on earth, it is not intended to deny Its reality or essential identity with His mortal Body, but a mystery is indicated, a spiritual state and a spiritual presence.

When Æcolampadius, after being a priest and religious of the order of St. Bridget, became first a disciple of Luther and afterwards with Zwingle founder of the Sacramentarian heresy, he attempted to defend his new views and give them a ground in antiquity by explaining away the language used by the holy Fathers about the Real Presence. His opponent, Blessed Cardinal Fisher, was so indignant at the impudent perversions to which Æcolampadius resorted, that he exclaimed, "Why, by such means you might as easily prove that you yourself never held the Real Presence, and might explain away the sermon which is published a few years back in its defence; for certainly you said nothing stronger or clearer than has been said by the Fathers whom you distort." Blessed Fisher was quite right. He who undertakes to prove that St. John Chrysostom did not hold the doctrine of Transubstantiation might as successfully maintain the same thing of Bossuet. And he who would deny that the Anglo-Saxon Church held on the subject of the Eucharist the doctrines afterwards defined by the Council of Trent, might also deny that the Council of Trent defined the doctrines now held by Roman Catholics.

KING HENRY VIII. AND THE ROYAL SUPREMACY.*

HENRY VIII. ascended the throne on April 22, 1509, and married, a few months later, by dispensation granted by Pope Julius II., Catherine of Arragon, the widow of his elder brother Arthur, a lady of singular virtue. But some years after, the King, tired of his wife, who had given him no surviving male issue, and in love with Anne Boleyn, affected to have scruples about his marriage, and solicited the Pope for a divorce from Catherine, on the ground that the Papal dispensation through which they had married was invalid. The cause of the divorce was a failure, and Henry determined to take the law into his own hands. There is still in existence a letter of instruction, signed by the King, to Gardiner, the King's agent at Rome, in which it is said: "The King is loth to recur to any remedy except the authority of the See Apostolic [the Pope] if he can find there favour answering to his merits;"† but he had not found the "favour" he expected—in other words, license for bigamy—so he had recourse to another remedy, his own authority.

Wolsey, to whom the King attributed the failure of his cause, was disgraced, and was charged with having violated the Statute of Præmunire by acting as Legate of the Pope. This statute was passed in 1373, during the reign of Richard II., and was intended to prevent benefices being granted by the Pope without the consent of the Crown. An arrangement was arrived at between the Papal Court and the Crown, and this statute practically passed into disuse. Each Archbishop of Canterbury was successively Legate of the Holy See, without a word of

---

* In connection with this subject it would be well to read also the pamphlet *Mr. Collette as a Historian*, by the Rev. Sydney F. Smith. Catholic Truth Society. Price 1d.

† *Letters and Papers, Foreign and Domestic, of the reign of Henry VIII.*, vol. iv. n. 5270.

(54)

objection on the part of the Sovereign. But in Wolsey's case this indictment was singularly unjust; for Wolsey had been appointed Legate at the expressed desire of the King, and had acted throughout as the King's agent, and under the King's direction. He had committed no fault save that of failure. However, Wolsey knew, better than any man, the King's nature, and that his only chance of escape was to yield. Accordingly, he pleaded guilty, threw himself on the King's mercy, and resigned all his benefices and possessions into the King's hands. He died a few months after; but the consequences of the offence with which he had been charged, and which, for reasons of prudence, he had admitted, did not die with him. By the advice of Thomas Cromwell, it was argued that the clergy, by submitting to Wolsey's authority as Legate, had become partakers of his crime, and were therefore subject to the same penalties, namely, imprisonment at the King's pleasure, and the forfeiture of the whole of their possessions to the Crown; the law officers were therefore directed to make out an indictment against the *whole body* of the clergy in the Court of King's Bench.

But Henry was not acting merely out of revenge, nor merely out of avarice; he was hatching a deep plot to get the whole ecclesiastical power into his own hands. Cromwell had persuaded him that the opinion of the learned on the question of the divorce was entirely in the King's favour; nothing was wanting but the approbation of the Pope: but if that approbation was not to be had, was the King therefore to forego his rights? At present, he said, England was a monster with two heads, but were the King to take the power now usurped by the Pope into his own hands, everything would be well, and the clergy, *finding that their lives and possessions were at the King's mercy*, would be ready enough to do his will.* Collier says: "There was more than money required of the clergy. The King, perceiving the process of the divorce move slowly at Rome, and the issue look un-

* Lingard, vol. vi. c. 3.

promising, projected a relief another way. To this purpose he seems to have formed a design of transferring some part of the Pope's pretensions upon the Crown, and setting up an ecclesiastical supremacy. And now, having gotten the clergy entangled in a *præmunire*, he resolved to seize the juncture and push the advantage."*

Accordingly when, on Feb. 7, 1531, the Convocation of Canterbury hastily assembled and offered the King a present of £100,000,† as purchase money for a free pardon, the present was, to their surprise, refused, unless in the decree by which the sum was voted a clause was inserted acknowledging the King as *sole protector and supreme head of the Church and clergy of England*. Convocation, crushed as it was by the penalties hanging over it, resisted the insertion of this clause; and for three days, negotiations were carried on between the King and Cromwell, through Thomas Boleyn, Viscount Rochford, father of Anne Boleyn, on the one hand, and the bishops on the other. The King also sent for some of the bishops, and promised them, on the word of a King, that if Convocation would acknowledge him as supreme head of the Church of England, he would never by virtue of that grant assume to himself any more power, jurisdiction, or authority over them than other kings had done before him; nor would he take upon himself to make or promulgate any spiritual law, or exercise any spiritual jurisdiction, nor yet by any kind of means intermeddle with them in altering, changing, or judging of any spiritual business. Soon after, Boleyn and the other lords who were acting for Henry came again to Convocation, and repeated what the King had told these Bishops, adding that anyone who should now oppose the King on this point must needs show a great distrust in his majesty's words after he had made so solemn an oath. The clergy were now, for the most part, giving way, and disposed to grant the King's demand, but Fisher, Bishop of Rochester, utterly refused, and besought Convocation to consider what mischief might be

---

* Collier ii. 62. † Equal to quite £1,000,000 at the value of our day.

brought upon the whole Church of Christ by this unseemly and unreasonable grant made to a temporal prince, which had never yet been so much as demanded before, nor could be within the power of any temporal ruler. "And therefore," said he, "if ye grant the King's request in this matter, it seemeth to me to portend an imminent and present danger at hand: for what if he should shortly after change his mind, and exercise in deed the supremacy over the Church in this realm? Or what if he should die and his successor challenge continuance of the same? Or what if the crown of this realm should in time fall to an infant or a woman that shall still continue and take the same name upon them? What then shall we do? Whom shall we sue? or where shall we have remedy?" The King's counsellors replied that the King demanded no more than might be allowed by the law of God, *quantum per legem Dei licet*, and they again reminded the clergy of the King's oath: then, as the holy bishop confuted their arguments, they left in great anger, saying, that whoever would not grant the King's request was not worthy to be accounted a true and loving subject.

Then the Bishops and other members of Convocation, fearing the King's anger, resolved to give way and to acknowledge him as supreme head of the Church of England, trusting to his kingly word that he would make no wrong use of the title granted. The Bishop of Rochester, however, again stood to the front; and seeing that they were fully resolved on compliance and that he was unable to change their minds, insisted that the words *quantum per legem Dei licet*, "as far as the law of God allows," should be inserted in the grant.* This was done, and the King seeing that he could not obtain the grant without this condition, had to be content with it, and pardoned the clergy their offence on their promise to pay him £100,000.†

* Dr. Lingard says *(Ibid.)* : "It is plain that the introduction of the words *as far as the law of Christ will allow*, served to invalidate the whole recognition; since those who might reject the King's supremacy could maintain that it was not allowed by the law of Christ."

† Dr. Hall's MS. See *Blessed John Fisher*, by the Rev. T. E. Bridgett, C.SS.R.

But it must not be thought that in allowing the King the title of Supreme Head of the Church of England that Convocation committed itself to an acknowledgment of the supremacy as it was understood later on, nor that they had revolted from their allegiance to the See of Rome. In the whole course of the discussion there is no mention of the See of Rome. The clergy objected to the title asked for, because it was vague and hitherto unheard of, and because they feared that Henry might use it to encroach upon the liberties and privileges of the English Church. Neither was there any formal decree by which this headship was acknowledged. It was merely by a clause inserted in the address to the King. In this address they ask pardon for any penalties incurred and offer their gift as an act of gratitude to the King for writing against Luther and for other acts in favour of the Church. After the words "English Church and clergy" comes the following clause: "Of which we recognise his majesty as the singular protector, the only and supreme lord, and, as far as the law of Christ allows, even the supreme head."

When this form was proposed in Convocation, the Archbishop, Warham, begged of the prelates assembled to allow it to pass, adding that no one was obliged to speak his mind, and that silence would be taken for consent; on this, some one present exclaimed: "Then we are all silent." No one spoke further, and it was recorded in the minutes of the Convocation that the decree granting the present of £100,000 to the King (in which decree appeared this clause on the supremacy) had passed unanimously.*

Thus the Royal Supremacy, in a vague and undefined sense, was acknowledged by the Southern Convocation. At York the Northern Convocation met under the presidency of Archbishop Warham, for the See of York was vacant through the death of Cardinal Wolsey, and a decree voting a present of £18,000 to the King, in which decree was the same clause admitting the Royal Supremacy, was proposed. Tunstall, Bishop of

* Wilkins, iii. 725.

Durham, alone had the courage to speak out. He not only voted against the recognition, but made a spirited and plain-spoken protest which, at his desire, was recorded in the acts. He protested against the title, not because it was a violation of the rights of the Pope, but because it was too vague, and, though capable of a true and right meaning, yet might also bear a false meaning which evil-minded persons would take advantage of. But notwithstanding his protest, the decree was passed.

The clergy soon regretted the step they had taken. Mr. Gairdner says:[*] "It was repented of almost as soon as made, for however theoretically defensible might be the title to which they had agreed, and whatever pains they might have made to guard against misconstruction, the clergy could not but feel the moral disadvantage at which they now stood in having yielded at all. Yet they were altogether helpless. Under the existing law of *præmunire* they were at the King's mercy. . . . . The clergy, ground down to the last extremity, were anxious that the bishops should retract in Parliament the acknowledgment of the Supremacy made in Convocation, and threatened that unless this was done they would not pay a single penny." Chapuys, the ambassador of Charles V. in London, wrote to the Emperor:[†] "The clergy are more conscious every day of the great error they committed in acknowledging the King as sovereign of the Church, and they are urgent in Parliament to retract it, otherwise they say they will not pay a penny of the 400,000 crowns. What will be the issue, no one knows."[‡] A protest against any encroachments on the liberties of the Church or on the authority of the Holy See, signed by a great number of the clergy of both pro-

---

[*] *Letters and Papers, Foreign and Domestic, of the reign of Henry VIII.*, vol. v. Preface, p. xvi. Of Mr. Gairdner's research and his strict impartiality in this important work one cannot speak too highly.

[†] March 22, 1531, ap. Gairdner.

[‡] The Bishops had, indeed, great difficulty in collecting the money, and on one occasion Stokesley, Bishop of London, was nearly killed.

vinces, was presented to the King; and a few months after, "Archbishop Warham, to atone for what he had done in Convocation, drew up a solemn protest against all enactments made in that Parliament in derogation of the Pope's authority, and of the independence of the clergy."*

In January of the year 1534, Parliament, which was now completely under the management of the King and his minister, Cromwell, enacted that no canons or decrees should be made by Convocation without the King's consent; that appeals might be made from the bishops to the Court of Chancery, but not to the Pope; that bishops should be made and consecrated without the leave of the Pope; that dispensations usually obtained from Rome should be obtained from the Archbishop of Canterbury, and that all payments hitherto made to Rome, as first fruits of benefices, should cease.

After this, the King required all the clergy, both secular and regular, to take the oath of succession, at the same time making a declaration that the Bishop of Rome had no more authority in England than any other foreign bishop, and that the King was supreme head of the Church of England—the saving clause "as far as is allowed by the law of Christ" being omitted. To refuse to take this oath was misprision of treason and punishable by perpetual imprisonment and forfeiture of all property. This oath was subscribed to by the greater part of the clergy, and a formal declaration against the authority of the Pope was obtained from both Convocations and from the universities. Further, in the autumn of the same year, 1534, Parliament enacted that the King and his heirs should be taken and reputed the only supreme heads on earth of the Church of England (again the saving clause was omitted), and to wish or will maliciously by word or work to deprive the King of this title was made high treason. Then followed "a series of appalling executions" (we are quoting from Mr. Gairdner†), "which completely subdued in England all

* Gairdner, *Ibid.*; Wilkins, iii. 746.
† *Letters and Papers*, &c., vol. viii. preface.

spirit of resistance, while abroad it filled the mind alike of Romanists and of Protestants with horror and indignation. That the nation disliked the change [of religion] as it disliked the cause of the change [the divorce], there can be very little doubt. On no other subject during the whole reign have we such overt and repeated expressions of dissatisfaction with the King and his proceedings." Mr. Green,* speaking of this period, says: "A reign of terror, organized with consummate and merciless skill, held England panic-stricken at Henry's feet."

We may sum up briefly what has been said on the subject of the Royal Supremacy as follows: (1) It was the King, not the clergy, who was the first and chief mover; (2) the motive was, not the desire of religious reformation, but the desire of a divorce from his lawful wife; (3) nothing against the Pope's authority was desired or even contemplated by Convocation; the renunciation of the Pope's authority was not insisted upon by the King until three years after; (4) the consent of the clergy was extorted by fear of the severest penalties, it was given in silence, unwillingly, and against their convictions, and repented of as soon as given; (5) obedience was enforced by the most cruel laws, notwithstanding which many of the noblest in the country refused to acknowledge the King as head of the Church, even though they knew that they would have to pay for it with their lives.

W. H. COLOGAN.

* *Short History of the English People*, c. vi.. See also *How Henry VIII. robbed England of her Ancient Faith*, Catholic Truth Society.

CATHOLIC TRUTH SOCIETY, 18, West Square, London, S.E.
[*Price* 2s. per 100.]

POPERY ON EVERY COIN OF THE REALM!

"BLESS my soul!" says honest John Bull, "what's this? Popery on the coin of the realm! Popery on a good English sovereign, on an English shilling, on an English penny! I don't believe a word of it."

"Nevertheless it's a fact. Every coin of the realm,—gold, silver, copper, from the biggest to the smallest, from the bulky crown-piece to the diminutive threepenny bit,—every single one without exception bears on its face a relic of Popery."

"Dear me! can it be possible?"—closely scanning a shilling drawn from the depths of his breeches pocket.—"No. I can't see it. There's neither cross nor image— Oh! Ah! You don't mean to say the image of our gracious Queen is Popery? I know images are rather Popish; but surely the image of her Majesty isn't?"

"No, my friend. The image of her Majesty is perfectly innocent of the charge of Popery. It's not in the image at all."

"Well, sir, where is it? Show it me. That's a good English shilling, and I say there's no mark of Popery on it."

"Look at the head side, and read the words printed round it."

"VICTORIA—Hum! Ah! It's Latin or some other lingo. I can't make much of it."

"Yes; it's Latin. These are the words:—VICTORIA DEI GRATIA BRITANNÆ REGINA: F: D: And this is the English of them:—Victoria by the grace of God Queen of England—"

"Well, there's no Popery about that. She *is* Queen of England by the grace of God, and she doesn't thank the Pope for it."

"But wait a bit. What about the two letters F. D.? Do you know what they mean?"

"No. I never took much notice of them before. What do they mean?"

"Well, they stand for two more Latin words, *Fidei Defensor*, which means *Defender of the Faith*."

"And so she is, God bless her, the Defender of the Faith. Isn't she the Head of the Church, and isn't she ready to defend it against the Pope or anyone else?"

"Yes, she is the head of your English Protestant Church; and I have no doubt she would be prepared to maintain it against all enemies. But is it not strange that she should make use of a title which was conferred by the Pope, and which means *Defender*—not of the *Protestant Faith*, but—of the *Roman Catholic Faith*."

"What! The Queen—her Gracious Majesty wear a title given by the Pope! Defender of the Roman Catholic Faith! What can you mean?"

"I mean just what I say. That title, *Defender of the Faith*, was given by the Pope to one of the sovereigns of England many years ago. And you can see how proud they are of it from the way they make use of it ever since. Queen Victoria is the 16th English sovereign who has borne that title! and you see it is the only title besides that of *Queen of England* she thinks it worth while to put on her coinage. In other words, her proudest title, after *Queen of England*, is that given by the Pope, *Defender of the Faith*."

"Given by the Pope, you say;—this title *Defender of the Faith* given by the Pope! I don't understand it at all."

"Well, it was this way. In the year 1520 Luther began the *Reformation*, as you call it, which was simply a revolt against the teaching and authority of the Catholic Church and the Pope: for I may remark in passing that Luther was a Roman Catholic priest and a monk for many years before he started as a reformer and founded the Protestant Church. Well, when Luther began his revolt, the religion of all the civilized world was Roman Catholic. England, for instance, was Roman Catholic from sea to sea; and the Pope had no more devoted children than the noblest Englishmen of the day."

"Oh, come now! You don't expect that I'm going to believe that, do you?"

"Wait a little. May be what I'm going to tell you will convince you. When Luther began to preach against the Catholic Church, good Catholics, all over the world, were shocked beyond measure at his teaching, and men of learning in every country wrote and spoke against him. It was not merely the Pope and the priests that opposed him, but very many educated laymen came forward as defenders of the old faith against the new. Among these was the King of England, Henry VIII."

"Henry VIII.! Why, I thought he was one of the staunchest Protestants that ever lived."

"Well, perhaps Protestantism can claim the last and worst part of his life; but in his earlier and better years, both as prince and king, he was a staunch Catholic. What I am going say will prove it. Henry was one of those Catholic laymen who came forward to refute Luther's heretical teachings; and with the aid (so it was said) of a learned and holy bishop, who had been his tutor and guardian and was now one of his councillors, Dr. Fisher, Bishop of Rochester, he drew up a very able and powerful defence of the Catholic Faith against Luther. This was the title of the work:—'A Defence of the Seven Sacraments against Martin Luther, by Henry, the eighth of his name, the most potent King of England and France and Lord of Ireland. A.D. 1521.'"

"Here are a few passages from this famous work:—

"*(a)* In the introduction he says:—'O what happy times were those when Holy Church wanted no defenders, since she had no enemy to contend with. But, alas! now-a-days one appeared who, concealing his satanic malice under the cloak of zeal for truth, and urged on by hatred and anger, vomits forth his viperous venom against the Church. Would to God that every soul renovated in the life-giving waters of baptism and redeemed by the blood of Christ, the old man and the child, the priest and the king, could arise to combat this ungrateful and impious wretch!'

"*(b)* In the course of the work he speaks thus of the

authority of the Pope :—' Do you (Luther) dare to deny that Christendom looks on Rome as her common mother? Even to the utmost extremities of the world everyone bearing the name of Christian inclines in humble submission to Rome. If that power which Rome claims for herself came neither from God nor man, did Rome usurp it? Did Rome steal it? When? Tell us, if you can; open the pages of history and consult them. But if that power be so ancient that its beginning is lost in the obscurity of time, then you should know that it is an established axiom of human laws that all possession, the source of which cannot be traced, is legitimate ; and that by the unanimous consent of all people it is forbidden to touch that which time has confirmed.'

"*(c)* Here is how he defends Confession of sins to a priest and Absolution, which Luther had ridiculed :— 'With regard to the power of the keys, I take no other argument but this. Luther asserts that the words of institution (St. Matthew xviii. 18) apply to the laity as well as the priesthood ; this Bede denies : which of them do you believe? Luther says yes; St. Ambrose says no : which do you believe ? Luther affirms ; the Catholic Church denies : which do you believe ?'

"*(d)* Here is how he speaks of Tradition and the authority of the Church in matters of faith :—'Without Tradition you are not certain that there is one Gospel extant. If the Church had not told us that the Gospel of St. John was the Gospel of St. John we should not have known that it was the work of the apostle, for we were not standing by his side when he wrote it. Why then do you not believe the Church when she tells you, —'This is what Jesus Christ has done ; these are the Sacraments He has instituted ; this is what the Apostles have handed down to us ;'—as you believe her when she says, 'This is what St. Matthew or St. Mark has related.'

"*(e)* He describes Luther as—' An audacious writer who puts himself above all law, despises our doctors, and from the pinnacle of his greatness laughs at the living lights of our Church, and insults the majesty of our pontiffs, traditions, dogmas, morals, canons, the faith and even the Church herself.'

"*(f)* This is how he concludes his work:—'All other Christians, I beseech, and by the bowels of Christ, whose faith we profess, I entreat, to turn their ears from his impious words, not to nourish schisms and strife, especially at this time, when Christians ought especially to be united against the enemies of Christ. Let them not listen to the insults and detractions against the Vicar of Christ' (the Pope) 'which the rage of this friar pours out. Let them not stain with impious heresies the hearts that are consecrated to Christ.'

"Here then you have Henry attacking Luther and the Protestants, and defending the Catholic Church and its doctrines, the authority of the Pope, the Seven Sacraments of the Catholic Church, Confession and Absolution of sins, the necessity of Tradition, and other points of Catholic faith. Now what do you say of Henry's religion?"

"Well, if all this be true, I can't deny that Henry was a Papist."

"And Henry's subjects as well. For look back at the second extract given above *(b)*, and notice how he speaks of all Christendom looking on Rome as a common mother, and everyone bearing the name of Christian, even to the utmost limits of the world, inclining in humble submission to Rome. Evidently Henry's own subjects must have been included in this description.— If, then, it is a fact that Henry wrote that work, it is also as you say, a fact that Henry and his subjects were all staunch Roman Catholics. Isn't that so?"

"Well, I-don't see how I can escape admitting that. But how am I to be sure he did write such a work?"

"Oh! there are many copies of it in existence. It was first printed in London and afterwards at Antwerp, Paris, Rome, and other places. Copies were sent to all the principal courts of Europe and to the universities. Many of these copies are still to be seen in the great libraries. Moreover, two copies engrossed on parchment and signed by Henry himself, and bearing the arms of

England on the title-page, were sent by special messenger to the Pope; and these are still in the Vatican library. The printed copies have a small coloured frontispiece representing Henry on his knees presenting his work to the Pope. The work is dedicated to the Pope; and on the last page are two lines of Latin verse to this effect,—' Henry, King of England, sends thee, Leo X., this his work, as a pledge of fidelity and friendship.' Along with the work Henry sent a Latin letter written with his own hand, which is also in the Vatican library. After telling how he was filled with indignation at hearing of the conduct and teaching of Luther, how he was at once impelled by his love for the Holy Apostolic See to turn all his attention to stopping the spread of the evil, and how he had called upon the German sovereigns to unite in crushing this revolt against the Church, he concludes :—' But not satisfied with these proofs of our zeal for the Catholic Faith and our devotion to the Apostolic See, we resolved to show by our own written words what we thought of Luther and his detestable books, thus to make it clear to all that we would be ever ready to defend and protect, as well with the pen as with the sword, the Holy Roman Church. Moreover we thought that this first effort of ours should be dedicated and consecrated to none other than to your Holiness . . . . and we shall consider its value greatly increased if it meets with your Holiness' approval.

'Your Holiness' most devoted and obedient Son,
'HENRY,
' By the Grace of God, King of England and France, and
'Lord of Ireland.
' From our Palace at Greenwich, May 21st, 1521.'

" We have also another letter of Henry's to Luther in which he speaks of him as one who had—' mocked at the Catholic Church, ridiculed the Fathers and holy Apostles, blasphemed the Saints and the Blessed Mother of God, and insulted the Lord Himself.'—But I think I need not go any further. What do you say now?

Have I proved that Henry was a Roman Catholic (or, as you are fond of expressing it, a Papist), and that he ruled over a Catholic people?"

"Well, I think you have got me pretty tight anyhow. I don't clearly see my way out of it. But what about the F. D.? We seem to have got away from that."

"Yes, so we have; but we can now settle it very easily. The title of *Defender of the Faith* was conferred by Pope Leo X. on Henry as a reward for his defence of the Catholic faith against Luther. The Papal Bull (as such documents are called) conferring the title is still in the British Museum, as also an autograph letter from the Pope, praising Henry and his work in the highest terms. Henry, to show his gratitude, wrote again to the sovereigns of Europe, calling upon them to put down Luther by force if necessary; and in signing his name he adds to it the title he had just received. Henry indeed afterwards renounced his allegiance to the Catholic Church because the Pope would not allow him to put away his wife and marry another; but even then he was still proud of his title of *Defender of the Faith*. The title was given to Henry personally, without the right of leaving it to his successors. Yet in 1543, some years after his revolt from the Pope, Henry had an Act passed, uniting the title of Defender of the Faith with that of Supreme Head of the Church of England and Ireland, and annexing these titles for ever to the Crown; and Henry's Protestant successors on the English throne down to her present Most Gracious Majesty have, each in turn, styled themselves *Defender of the Faith*.

"Now I think I have pretty clearly shown that there is Popery on the face of every coin of the realm. In fact every coin ought to be for an Englishman a sort of sign-post, directing him back to the old way in which his fathers trod. The F. D. upon it ought to remind him that less than four centuries ago this was a Catholic land, that its people from the king to the beggar were faithful children of the Roman Catholic Church. This would naturally lead him to ask,—How came the change? Was there any sufficient reason for it? If he went on to seek an answer to these questions, he would find that the change was brought about by the unbridled lust of a king who had become a tyrant, and would brook no restraint on his passions or power. He would find that it was not done by the people, nor with the sanction of the people; but on the contrary, in spite of the people, and only after many brave Englishmen and Englishwomen had nobly laid down their lives for the old faith of their fathers. And this perhaps would lead to the further question:—May not that old faith be the right faith after all, and may it not be a safer guide than so licentious and bloody an apostle as Henry VIII.?"

NOTE. The Protestant reader is invited to test the truth of the preceding in any good Histories of England. The facts and extracts are chiefly from Audin's Life of Henry VIII., and Lingard's History of England.

A LETTER
TO THE WORKING MEN OF ENGLAND.

———:o:———

THIRTEEN hundred years ago the Christian religion was brought to England by a good and holy man called Augustine.

Augustine was sent by a man, equally good and holy, called Gregory.

The religion preached by Augustine was the Roman Catholic religion, and the man Gregory, who sent him, was the Pope of Rome.

Augustine could not preach any other religion, because there was no other Christian religion known. The many different Protestant sects and religions, which are the stumbling-block and scandal of the present age, had not been invented. All the Christians in the world held but one Faith, and that was the Roman Catholic Faith.

England was, at the coming of Augustine, inhabited by a people called the Saxons, who had driven the older inhabitants, the Britons, into Wales and Cornwall. Many of the Britons were Christians and, of course, Roman Catholics, having received the Faith from Pope Eleutherius about one hundred and eighty years after our Lord's Ascension. But, owing to the misfortunes of war and their conquered condition, their religion had sunk to the lowest ebb, and they did nothing to spread it among the Saxons. Hence, when Augustine came, England was practically a heathen country. The success of Augustine's preaching was marvellous, and in a very short time the Saxons were converted to the Roman Catholic Faith.

For nearly a thousand years, this Faith, and this Faith only, was preached and practised in England. It covered the land with the beautiful cathedrals and churches which are still the wonder and admiration of mankind. It built Westminster Abbey, York Minster, the Cathedrals at Canterbury and Durham, and all those similar monuments of the Faith, Hope and Charity, of our ancestors, which are perpetual prayers to the God in whose honour they were raised. It fostered learning and the arts and sciences. It founded the Universities of Oxford and Cambridge. It took care of the poor and needy. Its monasteries, such as the Abbeys of Battle, St. Albans, Glastonbury, Bolton, and many others, too numerous to mention, were so many harbours of refuge for the starving and the destitute. The holy men and women who, as monks and nuns, renounced the world and all its pleasures, lived but to serve Almighty God. In ministering to the poor, they rendered the best of all service to Him who said: "Amen, I say to you, as long as you did it to one of these My least brethren, you did it to Me." Thus it was that the Roman Catholic Church won the proud title of the "Church of the Poor."

Three hundred years ago, a man ascended the throne of England called Henry VIII. His character is thus summed up by Charles Dickens, the well-known novelist, and a Protestant: "The plain truth is that he was the most intolerable ruffian, a disgrace to human nature, and

Working Men of England.

a blot of blood and grease upon the history of England." Upon the pretence of reforming alleged abuses in the monasteries, but in reality to satisfy his own avarice, he forcibly seized them, robbed them of the valuable gifts which had been made to them for centuries by a grateful people, turned the monks and nuns out upon the world, and sold the Church lands to his favourites.

At the same time, because the Pope would not give him leave to put away his lawful wife, Queen Katherine, and marry one of her maids of honour, a person of the name of Anne Boleyn, he assumed to himself the title of Supreme Head of the Church in England, and cut off England from the unity of the rest of Christendom. The English people were therefore separated from the Pope, who, as the successor of St. Peter, is the true Head and Chief Bishop under Christ of the whole Church upon earth. In his place they had forced upon them a self-made Pope, acting under no divine authority or guidance, swayed by the most degrading vices; a man who condemned all who disbelieved in him, or his opinions to a horrible death. The result was that, by the time he died a loathsome death, having married six wives and beheaded two of them, thousands of persons had suffered death during his reign of terror for their conscience' sake.

From this time (with the exception of the five years' reign of Queen Mary, whom Protestants delight to call "Bloody Mary," but who, with all her faults, was an angel of light in comparison with criminals such as Henry and Elizabeth) a long era of bitter persecution commenced for the Catholics. Under the

Acts of Parliament of the years 1563, 1571, 1581, 1585, 1587, and 1593, a second refusal to take the Oath of Supremacy (*i.e.*, that the Queen is "Supreme Governor as well in all spiritual or ecclesiastical things or causes as in temporal") was visited with death. It was death to hold any communication with the See of Rome; death to be reconciled or to reconcile any one to the Catholic Church; death for a priest to remain in the kingdom; death to maintain, relieve, or receive a priest; death to all Catholics, unable to pay the monthly fine of £20 for non-attendance at Protestant service, who neglected to quit the country. Besides this there were heavy fines and long imprisonment for saying or hearing Mass (that is, celebrating, or assisting at the celebration of the Communion service of the Catholic Church); and all dealings with landed property by Catholics were void. It may be mentioned that death under "Good Queen Bess" meant being hanged until you were half-dead, then to be cut down, and, while half-alive, to have your bowels torn out, and your body cut into four quarters. No wonder that, in the face of an ordeal as terrible as this, thousands consented to be anything or nothing. People are never at any time in a great hurry to lead self-denying religious lives, and when it involved a death so horrible as this, it was easy to find an excuse to stifle conscience. Nevertheless, many priests and people, during the reign of "that bright occidental star Queen Elizabeth, of happy memory," as she is called in the Preface to the Protestant translation of the Bible, met this death cheerfully rather than deny the Faith planted by Augustine a thousand years before.

And the poor? What did they do, deprived of the charity which had comforted and assisted them from the monasteries and convents? A very easy method was devised for getting rid of them. Elizabeth in July, 1595, directed a Commission to Sir Thomas Wilford, empowering him to arrest all vagrants and hang the most incorrigible. It need hardly be said that this Commission, and others of a similar nature, proved an effectual way of disposing of inconvenient paupers.

Persecution is an effectual weapon if wielded with sufficient determination. It has successfully stamped out many human institutions. Against the Church of God, however, it is powerless. The Divine Providence decreed that the light of Faith should be nearly extinguished in England—but not quite. For many years the penal laws against the Catholics were exercised in full force. The last martyrdoms took place in the reign of Charles II., from 1660 till 1685. The heavy fines and penalties imposed upon the handful of persons professing the ancient Faith were maintained until recent times. No Catholic could be a barrister, solicitor, doctor, officer under the Crown, or in the army or navy, or hold any public office. The Act of 1689, giving toleration to the Protestant dissenters from the Anglican Establishment, expressly excluded Catholics; and an Act of 1699 gave a reward of £100 to any one giving such information as should lead to the conviction of a priest saying Mass, and enacted that upon such conviction, the priest should be imprisoned for life.

At last the sense of fair-play which characterizes the English people, came to the aid of their harassed and distressed Catholic brethren. In the year 1829, the Catholic Emancipation Act was passed, removing most of the disabilities by which they had been so long oppressed, and restoring to them full rights of citizenship.

Since then, under the happy rule of our present gracious Sovereign, thousands have returned, and are returning, to the Faith of their forefathers. In the one fold of the Good Shepherd, our Lord and Saviour Jesus Christ, they worship Almighty God in union with the rest of the Christian world. Except in England and her colonies, Protestantism is an insignificant sect. In Germany, Denmark, Norway, and Sweden, which are its strongholds on the Continent, it is cold, lifeless, and' rotten with infidelity. In America it has developed a thousand eccentricities, and is unable to withstand the onslaughts of infidelity on the one hand, and the irresistible spread of Catholicism on the other.

To-day, in England, by the mercy of God, churches are gradually rising up, wherein the same religion is preached that was taught by Augustine before England was robbed of it by Henry VIII.

This religion is the Roman Catholic religion, against which you have heard so much. You have been told that Roman Catholics are idolaters; that they worship images; that they place the Blessed Virgin Mary above Almighty God; that they may not read the Holy Bible; that they would, if they could, burn all the Protestants; and a lot of other things that, if they were true, would prove Catholics to be very wicked people indeed. But are they true ? Come and see. You have only heard one side of the question as yet—the Protestant side.

Come and hear what the other side has to say. "Fair play is a jewel." The Catholic Church in England has not had fair play. She has been persecuted, oppressed, and vilified. She is beginning to lift up her voice once more. She looks to you, the working men of England, to strengthen that voice by granting her a fair hearing. Come and listen to what she has to say. There are few towns that do not possess a Catholic church or chapel. A humble little place perhaps—humble, it may be, as the wretched Stable at Bethlehem wherein your Saviour was born into the world which He had made, but still a place where you will hear the Faith preached which your forefathers received so gladly and suffered for so nobly. Come to the services held there. Listen to the sermons you will hear at these services. Perhaps at first you will not understand the services themselves. If this is so, don't give the whole thing up as a bad job. Stick to it. Inquire. Buy a sixpenny book called *Catholic Belief*, that you can get at any Catholic bookshop; or send to 21 Westminster Bridge Road, S.E., for a little twopenny book called *A Letter to the People of England on the Revival of the Catholic Faith in their midst*, and also ask for a list of little books especially intended to explain the teaching of the Catholic Church. Ask those among your friends who are Catholics (if you know any) to explain the services to you. Better still, go to the priest and say that you want to know about the Catholic religion. He will gladly explain everything to you. Don't be ashamed of going to church in your working clothes. Do not think that the Catholic Church is only for rich people who can afford fine clothes. The Catholic

Church is the Church of both rich and poor, but she is the Church of the poor especially. You—the working men of England—are particularly called to be the friends and followers of our Lord and God Jesus Christ; for when He was on earth He was a working man. Until His thirtieth year He worked with St. Joseph, His foster-father, as a carpenter at Nazareth. His first friends and followers, the fishermen at Galilee, were working men. St. Peter, the first Pope to whom He said: "Thou art Peter, and upon this rock I will build My Church, and the gates of hell shall not prevail against it," was a working man. St. John, His beloved disciple, who leant upon His bosom at the Last Supper, and who stood at the foot of the Cross whereon He died for love of you, was a working man. So were St. James and St. Andrew, who gave their lives for the Catholic Faith. Come and hear what the religion is of which you have been robbed. Come and hear your Lord and Master, your brother Workman, say to you, as He said to the working men of old: "Follow Me."

L. D.

NOTE.

The historical facts quoted in this pamphlet may be substantiated by reference to Bede's *Ecclesiastical History* (Catholic); Pearson's *History of England during the Early and Middle Ages* (Protestant); Hallam's *Constitutional History of England* (Protestant); and the Statutes of Henry VIII., Elizabeth, and the following reigns.

CATHOLIC TRUTH SOCIETY, 21 Westminster Bridge Road, S.E.
[Price One Halfpenny, or 2s. per 100.]
(Seventieth Thousand.)